~ *The*
# Separation *of*
# Church and State

WRITINGS ON A FUNDAMENTAL FREEDOM
BY AMERICA'S FOUNDERS

Edited by

Forrest Church

BEACON
150

Beacon Press
Boston

Beacon Press
25 Beacon Street
Boston, Massachusetts 02108-2892
www.beacon.org

Beacon Press books
are published under the auspices of
the Unitarian Universalist Association of Congregations.

07 06 05 04 8 7 6 5 4 3 2 1

This book is printed on acid-free paper that meets
the uncoated paper ANSI/NISO specifications
for permanence as revised in 1992.

Design and composition by Yvonne Tsang
at Wilsted & Taylor Publishing Services

LIBRARY OF CONGRESS CATALOGING-IN-PUBLICATION DATA

The separation of church and state : writings on
a fundamental freedom by America's founders /
edited with commentary by Forrest Church.— 1st ed.
p. cm.
Includes bibliographical references and index.
ISBN 0-8070-7722-4 (cloth : alk. paper)
1. Church and state—United States—History—
18th century—Sources. 2. Freedom of religion—
United States—History—18th century—Sources.
I. Church, F. Forrester II. Title.

BR516.S46 2004
323.44'2'0973—dc22
2004006382

Contents

FEB 20 2014

❧ Introduction ❧

One chapter in the saga of our country's birth—
the dramatic debate over church-state separation—illustrates the founders' gathering vision more
vividly than almost any other. It spans three decades,
from 1772 (with Samuel Adams's broadside linking
religious and civil liberty) to 1802 (with Thomas
Jefferson's declaration that, in the Bill of Rights, a
"wall of separation" has been built between church
and state). Starring several of the new nation's leading protagonists, it also sets the tone for their experiment in governance. During the course of this
debate, religious liberty becomes the cornerstone of
e pluribus unum—"out of many, one."

Arguments over church-state separation didn't end
once the language of state and national constitutions
was finally hammered out. They continue to this very
day, with partisans (from the pulpit to the oval office)
interpreting the founders' and framers' actual intent.
People ask, should a judge be permitted to express his
reverence for religious laws by posting the Ten Com-

mandments in his courtroom? Are "faith-based" ini-
tiatives appropriate when generated out of the White
House? Under the Constitution, can state or federal
prisoners be organized according to faith and given
special privileges for spiritual achievement? Should
we restore the Pledge of Allegiance to its original language by removing the phrase "under God?" Is there
a place for any kind of prayer in the public schools?
Does church-state separation discriminate against religion, or, to the contrary, is organized religion in-
creasingly trespassing on secular ground? Should
marriage rights be extended to all couples, regardless
of gender? And, finally, is the lack of any mention of
God or Christ in the Constitution intentional, or did
the founders assume that everyone understood that
the United States of America was a Christian nation?
With issues such as these dividing the American people right down the middle, to address them with better justified confidence we must reopen the first
chapter of our history.

How citizens today view the founders' intent is as
much a Rorschach test of our personal religious and
civic views as it is a true picture of what such men as
Thomas Jefferson, James Madison, and even George
Washington had in mind when they drew up their
blueprint for the nation and began building state and
federal institutions according to its design. On both
the religious right and the secular left, much contem-
porary confusion stems from an inability to distin-
guish between: 1) the universal spiritual values that

underlie the American experiment in democracy, and 2) the role assigned to government to advance those same values by protecting freedom of conscience and belief.

The American Revolution was not driven by the anti-religious pathos that powered the French Revolution a decade later. In the Declaration of Independence, its draftsman (our most secular founder) emphatically proclaims, "We hold these truths to be self-evident, that all men are created equal and endowed by their creator with certain inalienable rights." Citing as his authority "nature and nature's God," Thomas Jefferson establishes for liberty and equality a clear metaphysic, grounded in nature itself as part of the Creator's plan. The founders' professed goal was to establish a nation true to the spirit of divine law, a spirit some understood in Christian terms and others according to the canons of Enlightenment philosophy. These two streams met to affirm the dual imperatives of equality and liberty, best expressed in the above-mentioned motto of *e pluribus unum*. And the first liberty the founders endeavored to ensure— articulating in the First Amendment what already was enshrined in their hearts—was religious liberty. Sworn ("on the altar of God" as Jefferson put it) to protect freedom of conscience, they established a clear line of demarcation between church and state, not to abridge but to fulfill the nation's spiritual mandate.

One British observer, G. K. Chesterton, memorably defined America as "a nation with the soul of a church." His characterization is 100 percent half-right. By the founders' design, we embody both the soul of a church *and* a resolutely secular mind. I tell here the story of how this unique development in the history of governance occurred, highlighting, in their own words, its champions' understanding of the essential significance full religious liberty held then and continues to hold for the future of our nation.

As was true of the broader American struggle for freedom, the revolution that led to religious liberty was powered by two very different engines: one driven by eighteenth-century Enlightenment values, the other guided by Christian imperatives that grew out of the Great Awakening, a spiritual movement that spread like wildfire across the American colonies throughout the middle decades of that same century. The former movement, emphasizing freedom of conscience as both a political and a philosophical virtue, stressed freedom *from* the dictates of organized religion. The latter, stemming from a devout reading of the gospels (especially their proclamation of spiritual liberty from bondage to the world's principalities and powers), demanded freedom *for* religion. Those who embraced Enlightenment teachings included the men most responsible for drafting our foundational documents (Thomas Jefferson, John Adams, John Jay, James Madison, and Alexander Hamilton). And many so-called "New Light" or "Dissident" ministers formed what one Tory referred to as the "Black Regiment," stirring people up by preaching the gospel of liberty.

Introduction

Together, these seemingly opposite world-views collaborated brilliantly and effectively to establish the separation of church and state in America.

Though new in the annals of statecraft, the American experiment in religious liberty was not without foundation, both in British Common Law and Christian Reformation teachings. And certainly the quest for religious freedom was instrumental to early American colonization, beginning with the Pilgrims of Plymouth and the Puritans of Massachusetts Bay, many of whom crossed the Atlantic in order to practice their faith more freely. Nonetheless, Great Britain maintained a church establishment; the leading Reformers replaced long-standing ties between European governments and the Roman Catholic Church with a Protestant church-state connection; and the Puritans, as President Howard Taft once put it, "came to this country to establish freedom of their religion, and not the freedom of anybody else's religion." In fact, the first major reform of the church establishment in Massachusetts was imposed by England. In 1684, King James II temporarily revoked Massachusetts' royal charter, due to restrictions the Puritans had imposed on their fellow Protestants limiting religious freedom and the right to worship. To receive their charter back, the leaders of the colony had to cede to all Protestants within their jurisdiction the right to worship as they pleased.

By the time our chapter in the tale of growing religious freedom in America opens, the spirit of reli-

Introduction

gious liberty has already made great strides. In the vanguard were Rhode Island and Pennsylvania. The Reverend Roger Williams, a fiery Baptist with an inviolable conscience, bequeathed Rhode Island with a charter guaranteeing freedom of conscience to all its citizens. Williams considered it "against the testimony of Christ Jesus for the civil state to impose upon the soul of the people a religion, a worship, a ministry." Calling for "free and absolute permission of conscience," he was banished from Massachusetts in 1635, to establish complete religious freedom in Rhode Island the following year. Half a century later, William Penn established Western New Jersey and then Pennsylvania on many of the same liberal principles. Nonetheless, in the early eighteenth century the overwhelming majority of American citizens lived under an established state religion. The Anglican church held this franchise in Maryland, Delaware, North Carolina, South Carolina, and Virginia (and to a lesser extent, New York), with the Congregational Church established in Massachusetts, New Hampshire, and Connecticut. By the time our story begins in the 1770s, most notably Massachusetts and Virginia—commonwealths whose leading citizens proved instrumental to the Revolutionary cause and took leading roles in shaping the new nation—still levied taxes to support both the established church and its clergy. As the new nation began to take shape, the combustible combination of state laws supporting religion and leading citizens from these same states

xii

passionate in their advocacy for such laws' abolition turned Massachusetts and Virginia into the principal laboratories for church-state reform.

Throughout the following pages, this dramatic story unfolds, not without its moments of ambivalence. In Virginia, Patrick Henry (whose immortal words, "Give me liberty or give me death," became a rallying cry for the rebellion) was both a valiant champion of religious liberty and also among the most persistent supporters of an, albeit reformed, established church. George Washington (with Thomas Jefferson perhaps the most secular-minded of the founders) closes his presidency with a paean to the central importance of morality and religion for the future survival of the state. Jefferson's chief lieutenant, the diminutive and brilliant James Madison (principle policy wonk among the nation's architects), studied for the ministry, became a dogged secular advocate of church-state separation, and then, during his tenure as the nation's fourth president, reversed Jefferson's precedent by declaring national days of fasting and prayer.

Some of the figures you will meet here are less well-known: Baptist ministers Isaac Backus and John Leland for instance, and Presbyterian ministers Caleb Wallace and John Witherspoon (though Witherspoon, president of Princeton and a signer of the Declaration of Independence was a major player on the national scene). Each a devoutly Christian champion of church-state separation, their words serve as a continuing reminder of the danger any hint of collusion between church and state poses to the attainment and maintenance of full Christian liberty.

I arrange the following documents in chronological order, framing the debate with two writings that precede and follow it: the former, a ringing court summation by Patrick Henry in defense of three preachers charged with witnessing to heterodox religious views, and the latter, James Madison's bittersweet late-life reflections on the battle he and others waged for religious liberty, interlaced with his concerns about ongoing dangers that might jeopardize the integrity of church-state separation in the future. Between these bookends is a brief, yet complete basic library of the most illustrative and significant documents to emerge from the original church-state debate (including Madison's "Memorial and Remonstrance," Jefferson's "Statute for Religious Freedom in America," and selections from Washington's "Farewell Address."). In practical terms, perhaps the most important papers I include are six letters from President Washington to religious leaders affirming his sworn fidelity to church-state separation, and the 11th Article of the Treaty of Tripoli—presented by President John Adams and ratified by the entire U.S. Senate—which opens with the words, "As the government of the United States of America is not in any sense founded on the Christian religion...."

I follow these documents with an appendix: observations on the American experiment in granting religious liberty to its citizens written by a sympathetic British observer, the Unitarian minister Richard Price.

In my running commentary I attempt to bring these addresses, papers, statutes, and letters to life, weaving them into a single story by relating its chapters to one another as best I can. Whether I have succeeded in this endeavor or not, the documents stand on their own as vivid testimony to the passion, vision, and faith of these extraordinary citizens, the civic artists who forged our nation, entrusting to the care of succeeding generations the protection and further implementation of their ideals.

Before I turn to the documents themselves, one final observation: Advocates for a so-called return to the values upon which the United States of America was founded speak with heartfelt sincerity of the need to reestablish a Christian nation to restore the founders' vision. The arguments they raise are perhaps the clearest reminder that we must revisit our early history to recover—and thereby keep from betraying—the founders' original script.

❧ 1 ❧

In Defense of
Religious Liberty

Patrick Henry

The greatest revolutionary orator, Patrick Henry, learned his art from the storied pulpiteers of Hanover County, Virginia. Hanover was a hotbed of Presbyterian and Baptist dissenters in a colony where the Anglican Church was established by law. Though raised Anglican (his uncle was a clergyman, his father, a vestryman), Henry's oratorical style was more indebted to the dissenters' enthusiasm than to staid Episcopal propriety. One opponent likened his firebrand approach to that of "a Presbyterian clergyman, used to haranguing the people."

Henry's first major case turned on a matter of church and state. In 1763, serving in the Hanover County Courthouse, the twenty-six-year-old lawyer tackled a group of Anglican clergymen who were pe-

1

titioning the court for back compensation from the state to supplement their tax-generated income. The question grew out of a debate over how the state support of clergy should be reckoned, a matter that turned—strangely to our ears—on the price of tobacco (the medium of exchange by which tax assessments, though sometimes paid in cash, were then determined). Since 1662, clergy stipends had fluctuated with the market. In drought years the price of tobacco went up, and with it rose the clergy's fortunes. At times of great duress, their "livings" might increase as much as threefold. In response to the complaints of aggrieved taxpayers, whose suffering reaped a windfall for the established church, in 1755 the General Assembly passed an act standardizing clergy support by fixing the tax at two cents per pound of tobacco per year, regardless of the market price. After fierce lobbying, the king yielded to Anglican ecclesiastical lobbyists and countermanded this legislation, without specifying whether his decision was retroactive. Seizing on this ambiguity in the law, some clergymen petitioned the courts for back taxes.

Enter Patrick Henry. Colorfully branding these clerical plaintiffs as "rapacious harpies snatching from the hearth of their honest parishioner his last hoecake, from the widow and her orphan children their last milch cow," Henry turned the jury against them even as he underscored the moral contradictions implicit in any law that taxed parishioners more highly for clergy support when times were hard than when they were not. By overruling the Two Penny Act, which had been drafted to eliminate clerical windfalls, the king himself earned Henry's most scathing indictment. "From being the father of his people," the Sovereign had "degenerated into a tyrant, and forfeits all rights to his subjects' obedience."

Patrick Henry was far from anti-religious. Nor, as we shall later see, was he opposed to state support for clergy, so long as all faiths were treated equitably. He took particular cause with Baptist ministers who received no state support and sometimes were even fined for witnessing to their faith. Bailing poor dissenting ministers out of jail (for which he became famous), Henry found in the growing populist resistance to the alliance between pulpit and throne an emotional issue to help him drum up support for the revolutionary cause.

Direct repercussions from the mid-century revival known to historians as the Great Awakening (pitting "New Light" evangelists against "Old Light" representatives of established churches) reverberated in Virginia well into the 1770s, longer than in any other state. Religious freedom was costly to Virginia's dissenting preachers. Not only did they receive no state support in exchange for the religious assessments they too had to pay, but also, from 1768 to 1775, evangelical preachers got arrested quite regularly for "disturbing the peace." In one notable case—leading to the imprisonment of five Baptist preachers in Fredericksburg, Virginia in 1768—the prosecutor charged,

"May it please your Worships, these men are great disturbers of the peace; they cannot meet a man upon the road, but they must ram a text of scripture down his throat." The judge offered to stay their sentence on the condition that the defendants swear off preaching for a year and a day. Refusing to accept the condition placed on their freedom, instead they chanted hymns all the way from the courthouse to the jail.

The following summation (freely reconstructed, as were many of Henry's speeches, therefore suggestive of the spirit, rather than literally faithful to the letter of his actual words) is drawn from his *pro bono* defense sometime in the late 1760s or early 1770s of three dissenting preachers, who were charged by the Royal Governor for witnessing to their faith. The nineteenth-century historian James Parton describes Henry's impact on the jury as follows:

> Every eye was riveted upon him, and every mind intent; for all this was executed as a Kean or a Siddons would have performed it on the stage—eye, voice, attitude, gesture, all in accord to produce the utmost possibility of effect. Amid a silence that could be felt, he waved the indictment three times round his head, as though still amazed, still unable to comprehend the charge. Then he raised his hands and eyes to heaven, and in a tone of pathetic energy wholly indescribable, exclaimed, "Great God!"

MAY IT PLEASE your Worships, I think I heard read by the prosecutor, as I entered the house, the paper I now hold in my hand. If I have rightly understood, the king's attorney has framed an indictment for the purpose of arraigning and punishing by imprisonment these three inoffensive persons before the bar of this court for a crime of great magnitude,— as disturbers of the peace. May it please the court, what did I hear read? Did I hear it distinctly, or was it a mistake of my own? Did I hear an expression as of crime, that these men, whom your Worships are about to try for misdemeanor, are charged with— with—with what?

Preaching the gospel of the Son of God!

Great God!

May it please your Worships, in a day like this, when Truth is about to burst her fetters; when mankind are about to be aroused to claim their natural and inalienable rights; when the yoke of oppression that has reached the wilderness of America, and the unnatural alliance of ecclesiastical and civil power is about to be dissevered—at *such* a period, when Liberty, Liberty of Conscience, is about to wake from her slumberings, and inquire into the reason of such charges as I find exhibited here today in this indictment—if I am not deceived, according to the contents of the paper I now hold in my hand, these men are accused of *preaching the gospel of the Son of God!*

Great God!

May it please your Worships, there are periods in the history of man when corruption and depravity have so long debased the human character, that man sinks under the weight of the oppressor's hand— becomes his servile, his abject slave. He licks the hand that smites him. He bows in passive obedience to the mandates of the despot; and in this state of servility, he receives his fetters of perpetual bondage. But may it please your Worships, such a day has passed. From that period when our fathers left the land of their nativity for these American wilds—from the moment they placed their feet upon the American Continent—from that moment despotism was crushed, the fetters of darkness were broken, and Heaven decreed that man should be free—free to worship God according to the Bible. In vain were all their offerings and bloodshed to subjugate this new world, if we, their offspring, must still be oppressed and persecuted. But, may it please your Worships, permit me to inquire once more: For what are these men about to be tried? This paper says, *for preaching the gospel of the Saviour to Adam's fallen race!*

What laws have they violated?

The presiding judge ended the scene by saying:

"Sheriff, discharge these men."

❦ 2 ❦

The Rights of the Colonists

Samuel Adams

If Patrick Henry is widely regarded as the ablest political agitator in the southern colonies, in the north, Samuel Adams lays claim to the same title. Norman Cousins considered it "doubtful whether any American ever stood higher on a soapbox or used it to greater advantage." Adams served in the Massachusetts Assembly, was first to propose the establishment of a Continental Congress, went on to sign the Declaration of Independence, and was elected governor of Massachusetts in 1794. But it was his charter for independence, which anticipated the Declaration of Independence by four years and proved useful to the cause both at home and abroad, that left his most lasting mark.

Historians rightly stress the importance of eco-

nomic factors in documenting the growing rift between the colonies and the crown. And they freely
acknowledge the influence of liberal political philosophers from England, France, and especially Scotland. But the religious roots of revolution are not as
frequently acknowledged. At once radical and pious,
Adams combined in one person the political liber-
tarianism of John Locke's Enlightenment and the
Christian revival spirit of Jonathan Edwards' Great
Awakening (together, the principle sources for the
American revolutionary spirit). To him, the principles of political liberty and religious liberty were
inextricably intertwined. "The religion and public
liberty of a people are so intimately connected, their
interest are interwoven, and cannot exist separately,"
he said.

Sam Adams viewed Parliament's imposition of the
Stamp Act (a tariff imposed on all printed papers and
documents, including wills, newspapers, and playing
cards) with the same disdain that Patrick Henry held
toward the Royal countermanding of the Two Penny
Act. Both men perceived the relationship between
taxing authority and the established church as a collusion that might swiftly lead to an infringement of
religious freedom. "I could not help fancying that the
Stamp Act itself was contrived with a design only to
inure the people to the habit of contemplating themselves as the slaves of men," Adams wrote. On another occasion, he suggested that "revenue raised in

America, for ought we can tell, may be constitutionally applied towards the support of prelacy."

Such suspicions were fueled by a cadre of British Anglican missionaries, whose arrival in America seemed orchestrated to secure political as much as spiritual advantage for both miter and crown. Samuel Adams, who often displayed anti-Catholic bigotry, was not shy to paint the Anglicans with the same brush he used to tar the Catholics. His fear was that, even as Roman Catholic loyalty would tilt toward Rome (a belief that recurs throughout the nation's history), so would an Episcopate in America seal British sovereignty over American souls.

However exaggerated the fear of growing Anglican hegemony was, Episcopalian patriots in Virginia were sensitive to the same danger. In 1774, a young James Madison, then a post-graduate student of theology at Princeton studying the scriptural and historical relationship between civil and religious freedom under the direction of future patriot John Witherspoon, wrote (in a January 24 letter to his friend William Bradford, Jr.):

> If the Church of England had been the established [church] and general religion in all the northern colonies as it has been among us here [in Virginia], and uninterrupted tranquility had prevailed throughout the continent, it is clear to me that slavery and subjection might and would have been gradually insinuated among us. Union of religious sentiments begets a surprising

confidence, and ecclesiastical establishments tend to great ignorance and corruption; all of which facilitate the execution of mischievous projects.

John Adams (Sam's second cousin) saw a direct relationship between the colonists' wariness of royal infringement of their religious liberties and the consequent urge toward rebellion. Calling this connection "a fact as certain as any in the history of North America," he went on to claim that Anglican meddling in colonial affairs, "as much as any other cause, aroused the attention, not only of the inquiring mind, but of the common people, and urged them to close thinking on the constitutional authority of Parliament over the colonies." Adding to the immediacy of this concern, in 1774 the British Parliament expanded Quebec's boundaries and sanctioned the appointment of a bishop to oversee the spiritual lives of Canadian Roman Catholics. In Puritan New England this fomented not only anti-Catholic but also anti-Anglican bias, fanning colonists' fears that the Parliament might one day attempt to enforce Anglican hegemony over them.

By way of a historical footnote, following independence—mindful of the whiplash against both the Quebec Act and the Anglican proselytizers who had descended on the colonies shortly before the war—American Catholic leaders were swift to establish greater distance from Rome. Maryland's John Carroll, appointed by the Pope to serve as Superior to the

Catholic Mission in America shortly after the Revolution, made it clear that no American bishop could submit to having his and the church's affairs under foreign jurisdiction. The Holy See was understanding, and, for years thereafter, American Catholics chose their own bishops.

Sam Adams's greatest contribution to the revolutionary cause was "The Rights of the Colonists," which I excerpt below—one of three documents submitted in the Report of the Committee of Correspondence to the Boston Town Meeting on November 20, 1772. A tax collector himself, Adams might easily have inspired the loathing of his fellow colonists. Instead, he employed his knowledge of the tax code and his extensive professional contacts with Boston merchants to agitate for reform. Benjamin Franklin—noting that "All accounts of the discontent so general in our colonies have of late years been industriously smothered and concealed here" —published Adams's broadside in England, "[t]hat the true state of affairs there [in America] may be known, and the true causes of that discontent well understood."

❧ . . . . ❧

AMONG THE NATURAL rights of the colonists are these: first, a right to life; second, to liberty; third, to property; together with the right to support and defend them in the best manner they can.

These are evident branches of, rather than deductions from, the duty of self-preservation, commonly called the first law of nature.

• All men have a right to remain in a state of nature as long as they please; and in case of intolerable oppression, civil or religious, to leave the society they belong to, and enter into another.

• When men enter into society, it is by voluntary consent; and they have a right to demand and insist upon the performance of such conditions and previous limitations as form an equitable original compact.

• Every natural right not expressly given up, or, from the nature of a social compact, necessarily ceded, remains.

• All positive and civil laws should conform, as far as possible, to the law of natural reason and equity.

• As neither reason requires nor religion permits the contrary, every man living in or out of a state of civil society has a right peaceably and quietly to worship God according to the dictates of his conscience.

• "Just and true liberty, equal and impartial liberty," in matters spiritual and temporal, is

a thing that all men are clearly entitled to by
the eternal and immutable laws of God and
nature, as well as by the law of nations and all
well-grounded municipal laws, which must
have their foundation in the former.

In regard to religion, mutual toleration in the
different professions thereof is what all good and candid minds in all ages have ever practised, and, both
by precept and example, inculcated on mankind. And
it is now generally agreed among Christians that this
spirit of toleration, in the fullest extent consistent
with the being of civil society, is the chief character-
istical mark of the church. Insomuch that Mr. Locke
has asserted and proved, beyond the possibility of
contradiction on any solid ground, that such toleration ought to be extended to all whose doctrines are
not subversive of society. The only sects which he
thinks ought to be, and which by all wise laws are ex-
cluded from such toleration, are those who teach doctrines subversive of the civil government under which
they live. The Roman Catholics or Papists are ex-
cluded by reason of such doctrines as these....

The natural liberty of man, by entering into society, is abridged or restrained so far only as is necessary for the great end of society, the best good of the
whole.

In the state of nature every man is, under God,
judge and sole judge of his own rights and of the in-
juries done him.... [As Locke writes] "The *natural*

liberty of man is to be free from any superior power on earth, and not to be under the will or legislative authority of man, but only to have the law of nature for his rule...."

In short, it is the greatest absurdity to suppose it in the power of one or any number of men, at the entering into society, to renounce their essential natural rights, or the means of preserving those rights, when the great end of civil government, from the very nature of its institution, is for the support, protection, and defense of those very rights; the principal of which, as is before observed, are life, liberty, and property. If men, through fear, fraud, or mistake, should in terms renounce or give up any essential natural right, the eternal law of reason and the grand end of society would absolutely vacate such renunciation. The right to freedom being the gift of God Almighty, it is not in the power of man to alienate this gift and voluntarily become a slave.

The Rights of the
Colonists as Christians

These may be best understood by reading and carefully studying the institutes of the great Lawgiver and Head of the Christian Church, which are to be found clearly written and promulgated in the New Testament.

By the act of the British Parliament, commonly called the Toleration Act, every subject in England, except Papists, etc., was restored to, and reestablished in, his natural right to worship God according to the dictates of his own conscience. And, by the charter of this province, it is granted, ordained, and established (that is, declared as an original right) that there shall be liberty of conscience allowed in the worship of God to all Christians, except Papists, inhabiting, or which shall inhabit or be resident within, such province or territory. Magna Charta itself is in substance but a constrained declaration or proclamation and promulgation in the name of the King, Lords, and Commons, of the sense the latter had of their original, inherent, indefeasible natural rights as also those of free citizens equally perdurable with the other. That great author, that great jurist, and even that court writer, Mr. Justice Blackstone, holds that this recognition was justly obtained of King John, sword in hand. And peradventure it must be one day, sword in hand, again rescued and preserved from total destruction and oblivion.

❧ 3 ❧

Baptist Appeals for
Religious Liberty

Isaac Backus

Many patriots had a sharp eye for foreign abridgements of their religious liberty, but local infringement of the same rights registered less clearly, a contradiction that surfaced during the debate over taxation without representation that followed Parliament's imposition of the Stamp Act and other tariffs. If British Parliament's imposition of tariffs on subjects without a voice in Parliament was wrong, could it be right for a colonial Assembly to impose a tax on members of one faith that benefited only the clergy of another?

This question was posed by Isaac Backus, Baptist clergyman and church historian. A Mayflower descendent (born in Norwich, Connecticut, in 1724), Backus served his parish in Middleborough, Massachusetts, for sixty years until his death in 1806. Throughout the early years of his ministry, Massachusetts Baptists were repeatedly fined, whipped, and incarcerated for faith-related offenses. Backus himself spent a short time in jail for refusing to pay the annual assessment imposed in support of the established Congregational clergy (a law enacted in 1692). This sentence neither affected his convictions nor tempered his practice.

Thomas Jefferson would soon stress the importance of freedom *from* religion as a safeguard against coercion; in the original Baptist spirit, Backus placed his emphasis on freedom *for* religion, a freedom compromised by any form of state interference, however preferential. In such a view, church-state separation protects the church from the state, not the state from the church. Backus built his case for religious liberty —like Roger Williams before him—on a foundation of scriptural pietism. However much the persecutorial spirit had ebbed in Massachusetts over the intervening century and a half, Williams surely would have found the resistance Backus met to his cry for reform familiar.

Unlike in Virginia, where Madison and Jefferson eventually prevailed, in Massachusetts Backus did not. Nonetheless, the case he presented, especially in his lengthy tract, "An Appeal to the Public for Religious Liberty" (excerpted below) contains a strong rhetorical revolutionary-era argument for faith-based liberty. Illustrating his presentation with Biblical injunctions—for example, that Christ's Kingdom is not a "worldly" Kingdom—Backus went so far as to suggest that America could never become in spirit a true Christian nation until complete church-state separation had been secured.

Backus supported the American Revolution, which he and the members of his sect called "the new Reformation." Nonetheless, while serving as the Baptist agent at the 1774 Continental Congress in Philadelphia to present the Baptist case for religious freedom, he met a chorus of "patriotic" criticism. Charged with pressing the same suit on behalf of English Baptists (which he certainly, and consistently, had done), he was branded a traitor. A cry even went up for him to be sent to the gallows.

Soldiering onward, Backus finally won an audience with the Massachusetts delegation. There, he received a cool reception from both Sam and John Adams, the latter pointedly telling him that disestablishment of the church in Massachusetts was out of the question. Later that year, on December 9, 1774, Backus did manage to secure a resolution from the Massachusetts Provincial Congress, with the Congress's president, John Hancock, assuring him that Baptist grievances would be taken up at the next Massachusetts General Assembly. There, in Watertown, Massachusetts, the following July, he submitted language for legislation to this end, which, though considered, was finally tabled (both documents are reprinted below).

None of these setbacks dampened Backus's revolutionary ardor. Nor did they diminish his appreciation for the progress being made toward church-state separation at the national level. In 1787, when serving as a delegate to the Massachusetts State Convention called to ratify the U.S. Constitution, Backus commended the framers for excluding any reference to a religious test for public office: "Many appear to be much concerned about it; but nothing is more evident, both in reason and the Holy Scriptures, than that religion is ever a matter between God and individuals, and, therefore, no man or men can impose any religious test without invading the essential prerogatives of our Lord Jesus Christ."

⋙ • • • • • • • • • • • • • • • • • ⋘

I

*"An Appeal to the Public
for Religious Liberty"*

THE GREAT importance of a general union through this country, in order to [ensure] the preservation of our liberties, has often been pleaded for with propriety; but how can such a union be expected so long as that dearest of all rights, equal liberty of conscience is not allowed? Yea, how can any reasonably expect that he who has the hearts of kings in his hand, will turn the heart of our earthly sovereign to hear the pleas for liberty, of those who will not hear the cries of their fellow-subjects, under their oppressions? Has it not been plainly proved, that so far as any man gratifies his own inclinations, without regard to the universal law of equity, so far he is in bondage? . . . [I]t is impossible for any one to tyranize over others, without thereby becoming a miserable slave himself: a slave to raging lusts, and a slave to guilty fears. . .

Suffer us a little to expostulate with our fathers and brethren, who inhabit the land to which our ancestors fled for religious liberty. You have lately been accused with being disorderly and rebellious, by men in power, who profess a great regard for order and the public good; and why don't you believe them, and rest easy under their administrations? You tell us you cannot, because you are taxed where you are not represented; and is it not really so with us? You do not deny the right of the British parliament to impose taxes within her own realm; only complain that she extends her taxing power beyond her proper limits; and have we not as good right to say you do the same thing? . . . [W]herein you judge others you condemn your selves? Can three thousand miles possibly fix such limits to taxing power, as the difference between civil and sacred matters has already done? One is only a distance of space, the other is so great a difference in the nature of things, as there is between sacrifices to God, and the ordinances of men. This we trust has been fully proved.

If we ask why have you not been easy and thankful since the parliament has taken off so many of the taxes that they had laid upon us? you answer that they still claim a power to tax us, when, and as much as they please; and is not that the very difficulty before us? . . .

As the present contest between Great-Britain and America is not so much about the greatness of the taxes already laid as about a submission to their taxing power, so (though what we have already suffered is far from being a trifle, yet) our greatest difficulty at present concerns the submitting to a taxing power in ecclesiastical affairs. . . . And we have one difficulty in submitting to this power, which our countrymen have not in the other case: that is, our case affects the conscience, as their's does not: and equal liberty of conscience is one essential article in our charter, which constitutes this government, and describes the extent of our rulers' authority, and what are the rights and liberties of the people. And in the confession of faith which our rulers and their ministers have published to the world, they say, God alone is Lord of the conscience, and hath left it free from the doctrines and commandments of men, which are, in any thing contrary to his word; or not contained in it; so that to believe such doctrines, or to obey such commands, out of conscience, is to betray true liberty of conscience; and the requiring of an implicit faith, and an absolute blind obedience, is to destroy liberty of conscience and reason also. . . .

[I]f the constitution of this government gives the magistrate no other authority than what belongs to civil society, we desire to know how he ever came to impose any particular way of worship, upon any town or precinct whatsoever? And if a man has a right to his estate, his liberty, and his family, notwithstanding his non-conformity to the magistrates' way of worship, by what authority has any man had his goods spoiled, his land sold, or his person imprisoned, and thereby deprived of the enjoyment both of his liberty and his family, for no crime at all against the peace or welfare of the state, but only because he refused to conform to, or to support an imposed way of worship, or an imposed minister? . . .

Thus we have laid before the public a brief view of our sentiments concerning liberty of conscience, and a little sketch of our sufferings on that account. If any can show us that we have made any mistakes, either about principles or facts, we would lie open to conviction: But we hope none will violate the forecited article of faith so much, as to require us to yield a blind obedience to them, or to expect that spoiling of goods or imprisonment can move us to betray the cause of true liberty.

II
Action of the Provincial Congress, Cambridge, Massachusetts. in response to the Memorial Presented by the Reverend Isaac Backus

RESOLVED, That the establishment of civil and religious liberty to each denomination in the province is the sincere wish of this Congress; but being by no means vested with powers of civil government, whereby they can redress the grievances of any person whatever, they therefore recommend to the Baptist Churches that when a General Assembly shall be convened in this colony they lay the real grievances of said Churches before the same, when and where this petition will most certainly meet with all that attention due to the memorial of a denomination of Christians so well disposed to the public weal of their country.

By order of the Congress, JOHN HANCOCK, President. BENJAMIN LINCOLN, Secretary. A true extract from the minutes.

III
Memorial Submitted
(upon recommendations by the
Provincial Congress) to the
Watertown General Assembly

OUR REAL grievances are that we, as well as our
fathers, have from time to time been taxed on religious accounts where we were not represented; and
when we have sued for our rights, our causes have
been tried by interested judges. That the Representatives in former Assemblies, as well as the present,
were elected by virtue only of civil and worldly qual-
ifications is a truth so evident that we presume it need
not be proved to this Assembly; and, for a civil Legislature to impose religious taxes is, we conceive, a
power which their constituents never had to give, and
is, therefore, going entirely out of their jurisdiction.
Under the legal dispensation, where God himself
prescribed the exact proportion of what the people
were to give, yet none but persons of the worst character ever attempted to take it by force. How daring
then must it be for any to do it for Christ's ministers,
who says, "My kingdom is not of this world!" We be-
seech this honorable Assembly to take these matters
into their wise and serious consideration before Him,
who has said, "With what measure ye mete it shall be
measured to you again." Is not all America now ap-
pealing to Heaven against the injustice of being taxed

where we are not represented, and against being judged by men who are interested in getting away our money? And will Heaven approve of your doing the same thing to your fellow servants! No, surely.

We have no desire of representing this government as the worst of any who have imposed religious taxes; we fully believe the contrary. Yet—as we are persuaded that an entire freedom from being taxed by civil rulers to religious worship is not a mere favor from any man or men in the world, but a right and property granted us by God, who commands us to stand fast in it—we have not only the same reason to refuse an acknowledgment of such a taxing power here as America has the abovesaid power, but also, according to our present light, we should wrong our consciences in allowing that power to men, which we believe belongs only to God.

❧ 4 ❧

Colonial Declarations
of Rights

I. VIRGINIA DECLARATION OF RIGHTS
Drafted by George Mason

In addition to the Continental Congress, which drafted and ratified the American Declaration of Independence in July 1776, each of the former colonies passed its own distinctive declaration of rights during the early years of the Revolution. The first to do so was the Commonwealth of Virginia, whose delegates, gathering in Williamsburg, established a model both for the twelve other colonies (whom they called upon to do the same) and for the delegates meeting concurrently in Philadelphia.

Adopted by the Virginia Constitutional Convention on June 12, 1776, the Virginia Declaration of

Rights was drafted by George Mason, a wealthy Virginia plantation owner. Among the things that distinguished Mason from the great majority of his fellow planters was his outspoken opposition to slavery, the responsibility for which, together with Thomas Jefferson, he partially laid at the feet of the King for permitting the slave trade to flourish in the first place. Given the breadth of its inclusiveness, his First Article—"all men are by nature equally free and independent, and have certain inherent rights," itself a model for Jefferson's wording in the Declaration of Independence—led to tension at the Convention. Those who dismissed all claims to Black equality balked at language that seemed to suggest it. A qualifying amendment (establishing that "the means of acquiring and possessing property" were fundamental to the station of being "born free and equal") appeared to exclude slaves, who were themselves property. Only for this reason did the Declaration win approval. (Knowledge of this debate and its outcome may, to his credit, explain Jefferson's conspicuous omission of the word *property* from the preamble of the Declaration of Independence less than a month later. There, adopting another of Mason's phrases, he recast John Locke's familiar triad, "life, liberty, and property," to read, "life, liberty, and the pursuit of happiness.")

Throughout the Virginia Declaration, Mason's language anticipates not only the Declaration of Independence, but also the Bill of Rights. Near the end of his life, Jefferson went so far as to say, "the fact is unquestionable that the Bill of Rights" was "drawn originally by George Mason." In both language and spirit, the First Amendment is certainly anticipated in the twenty-sixth and final article of the Virginia Declaration, which explicitly addresses the imperatives of religious liberty. Some nineteenth-century historians suggest that it and the preceding article were afterthoughts—even that they were written, not by George Mason himself, but by Patrick Henry, who sat on the drafting committee. Outside Henry family hearsay, there is no independent evidence for this. We do know that James Madison (among the youngest of those present and here making his debut on the political stage) strongly objected to the original wording of Article XVI: "all men should enjoy *the fullest toleration in the exercise of religion* according to the dictates of conscience [italics mine]." Madison considered toleration a condescending virtue; to tolerate can mean "to abide with repugnance." As substitute wording, Madison proposed instead, *"the free exercise of religion."*

Here Patrick Henry does make an appearance in this chapter of our story (a fact that may have led to later exaggeration of his role). Madison sought someone of acknowledged stature to present his amendment on the floor, which—graciously, enthusiastically, and successfully—Henry did.

Although he studied theology and, for a short time, considered training for the ministry, James

Madison was liberal in his religious views. With his fellow Virginians Thomas Jefferson and George Washington, he grew up Episcopalian, but—like them in this also—never formally joined a church. The greatest legacy from his postgraduate year of theology at Princeton was a passionate, lifelong commitment to the separation of church and state.

⋙ • • • • • • • • • • • • • • • • • • • ⋘

A DECLARATION OF RIGHTS made by the representatives of the good people of Virginia, assembled in full and free convention: which rights do pertain to them and their posterity, as the basis and foundation of government.

SECTION I That all men are by nature equally free and independent and have certain inherent rights, of which, when they enter into a state of society, they cannot, by any compact, deprive or divest their posterity; namely, the enjoyment of life and liberty, with the means of acquiring and possessing property, and pursuing and obtaining happiness and safety. . . .

SECTION XV That no free government, or the blessings of liberty, can be preserved to any people but by a firm adherence to justice, moderation, temperance, frugality, and virtue, and by frequent recurrence to fundamental principles.

SECTION XVI That religion, or the duty which we owe to our Creator, and the manner of discharging it, can be directed only by reason and conviction, not by force or violence; and therefore all men are equally entitled to the free exercise of religion, according to the dictates of conscience; and that it is the mutual duty of all to practise Christian forbearance, love, and charity towards each other.

II. MASSACHUSETTS
DECLARATION OF RIGHTS
Drafted by John Adams

The man who was to serve as second president of the United States had more reverence for the stabilizing value of organized religion than he did for its actual tenets. John Adams shared his successor, Thomas Jefferson's, liberal religious views. His commitment to state support for organized religion was due to the church's positive moral influence on society, not for any contribution it might make to advancing the great issues of the day. When Georgia sent the Rev. John Zubly to the Continental Congress, observing that he was the first clergyman to have served there Adams dismissed all further clerical contributions by saying, "I can not but wish he may be the last." (Only one minister, the Rev. John Witherspoon of New Jersey, who played an influential role in church-state separation, signed the Declaration of Independence).

Adams's support for the church establishment in Massachusetts belies his deeply held, if somewhat overheated, concern that the Church of England might become an instrument of the Crown in America. In his "Dissertation on the Canon and the Feudal Law" (published in 1765, when he was a young lawyer), Adams describes collusion between the two as "a wicked confederacy between two systems of tyranny." His fear, even then, was that Great Britain might employ the conjoined powers of church and state to strip Americans of both civil and religious liberty. With respect to his own state's religious establishment, however, he expressed no such concern. In 1774, Adams dismissed Isaac Backus's petition for full religious liberty by suggesting that the Massachusetts system for state support of religion was not only too benign to occasion anyone's objection, but would stand forever—as long, he said, as the solar system itself. On the former point, he was correct: as church establishments went, the Massachusetts version was (at this point in its history) quite benign. On the latter point, he was mistaken, although the Massachusetts establishment *was* long-lasting, being the last to fall (in 1833, with assessments ending in 1806). A double irony for Unitarians, who have historically stood for church-state separation: Adams himself was a Unitarian, and, during its final years on the books, the last standing religious establishment in the United States lent more advantage to the Unitarian denomination than to any other.

By 1780, when Adams drafted and presented his Declaration of Rights to the Massachusetts Assembly, the language declaring people's fundamental liberty (Section I) had become formulaic. Sections II and III, however—the clauses that address religious liberty—look backward not forward.

Adams considered his model a liberal one. After all, state support for a single ecclesiastical communion was no longer mandated; every town would be free to distribute its religious tax assessments to all local teachers of religion, as long as they be Protestant. But to a purist like Backus, that a Baptist clergyman could now receive state aid did not make the continuing church-state collusion any less diabolic; furthermore, it weakened the Baptist case for claiming exclusion from payment of religious assessments.

Taken in its entirety, the Massachusetts Constitution (of which the "Declaration of Rights" constitutes the First Part) is the oldest constitution in the world still in active use.

≫ . . . . ≪

I

ALL MEN ARE born free and equal, and have certain natural, essential, and unalienable rights; among which may be reckoned the right of enjoying and defending their lives and liberties; that of acquiring, possessing, and protecting property; in fine, that of seeking and obtaining their safety and happiness.

II

It is the right as well as the duty of all men in society, publicly, and at stated seasons, to worship the Supreme Being, the great Creator and Preserver of the universe. And no subject shall be hurt, molested, or restrained in his person, liberty, or estate for worshipping God in the manner and season most agreeable to the dictates of his own conscience; or for his religious profession or sentiments; provided he does not disturb the public peace, or obstruct others in their religious worship.

III

As the happiness of a people and the good order and preservation of civil government essentially depend upon piety, religion, and morality; and as these cannot be generally diffused through a community but by the institution of the public worship of God and of public instruction in piety, religion, and morality: Therefore, to promote their happiness and to secure the good order and preservation of their government, the people of this Commonwealth have a right to invest their legislature with power to authorize and require, and the legislature shall from time to time, authorize and require, the several towns, parishes, precincts, and other bodies politic, or religious societies to make suitable provision, at their own expense, for the institution of the public worship of God and for the support and maintenance of public Protestant teachers of piety, religion, and morality in all cases where such provision shall not be made voluntarily.

And the people of this Commonwealth have also a right to, and do, invest their legislature with authority to enjoin upon all the subjects an attendance upon the instructions of the public teachers aforesaid, at stated times and seasons, if there be any on whose instructions they can conscientiously and conveniently attend.

Provided notwithstanding, that the several towns, parishes, precincts, and other bodies politic, or religious societies, shall at all times have the exclusive right of electing their public teachers and of contracting with them for their support and maintenance.

And all moneys paid by the subject to the support of public worship and of the public teachers aforesaid shall, if he require it, be uniformly applied to the support of the public teacher or teachers of his own religious sect or denomination, provided there be any on whose instructions he attends: otherwise it may be paid towards the support of the teacher or teachers of the parish or precinct in which the said moneys are raised.

And every denomination of Christians, demeaning themselves peaceably and as good subjects of the Commonwealth, shall be equally under the protection of the law; and no subordination of any one sect or denomination to another shall ever be established by law.

❧ 5 ❧

Memorial of the
Hanover Presbytery

Caleb Wallace

Though the Virginia Declaration of Rights
explicitly affirms religious liberty for all, the
government of Virginia continued to flirt with the
Anglican establishment. Due to the opposition of
delegates committed to continuing assessments in
support of the clergy, one amendment to the Declaration, presumably drafted by Madison, failed to win
acceptance at the June Convention: "No man or class
of man ought, on account of religion, to be invested
with particular emoluments or privileges." So, while
freedom *for* religion was ratified by the delegates,
freedom *from* religion (including the elimination
of assessments) was not. A rumor that assessments
would soon be reinforced led first to an anti-
assessment petition circulated by the Baptists that

garnered 10,000 signatures and then, shortly thereafter, to perhaps the most quietly persuasive religious
document to emerge during the course of the
founders' church-state debate—the "Memorial of the
Hanover Presbytery."

Hanover County, where Patrick Henry had grown
up, was among the most religiously pluralistic sections of old Virginia. In 1776, The Rev. Caleb Wallace, another recent Princeton graduate, was clerk of
the local Presbytery. Princeton, then known as the
College of New Jersey, was a Presbyterian school,
where the principle theologian of the Great Awakening, Jonathan Edwards, had briefly served as president. In 1768, the Reverend John Witherspoon
—signer of the Declaration of Independence and
outspoken advocate of church-state separation—
moved to Princeton from Glasgow, Scotland, to
assume the presidency. Witherspoon had tutored
James Madison in theology, instilling in him a passion for religious freedom and commitment to the
separation of church and state. Here again, this time
in the person of Caleb Wallace, Witherspoon's influence on the course of religious liberty in Virginia will
be felt.

As did Isaac Backus before him, Wallace asked
"[I]s it not as bad for our Assembly to violate their
own Declaration of Rights as for the British Parliament to break our charter?" Writing this in a letter of
condolence to the parents of a fellow Presbyterian
minister who was killed while serving the revolu-

tionary cause as a military chaplain, Wallace went on to say, "Our Transalpine Presbyterians . . . and indeed many dissenters in every part of the country [Virginia] were unwilling any longer to bear the burthen of an Establishment. These circumstances induced our Presbytery to take the lead and prepare a Memorial on the subject."

After drafting this memorial and receiving the blessings of his Presbytery, Wallace was deputized to go immediately to Williamsburg and petition the House of Delegates on their behalf. Remaining there for seven weeks and acting, almost certainly, through the agency of his fellow Princetonian James Madison, Wallace succeeded in getting his memorial placed before the legislature. Behind the leadership of Thomas Jefferson, who had returned from the Second Continental Congress in Philadelphia to assume his preferred place as a representative to the Virginia House, the delegates enacted a staying order that barred assessments for a year and declared "all penal or persecuting laws against any mode of worship, etc., null and void." (This order would be renewed annually until assessments were permanently ended.) Wallace was delighted, even though victory was both partial and far from permanent. The Assembly made it clear, first, that the question of assessments remained open (to be reconsidered more thoughtfully later) and also that the licensing of clergy and meeting houses would remain under the Assembly's purview.

Caleb Wallace went on to a distinguished career in law and education, moving to Kentucky in 1782, where he served in the legislature, helped lead the fight for statehood, and sat for more than twenty years on the Kentucky Court of Appeals.

❧ • ❦

TO THE HONORABLE the General Assembly of Virginia:

The Memorial of the Presbytery of Hanover humbly represents that your memorialists are governed by the same sentiments which have inspired the United States of America; and are determined that nothing in our power and influence shall be wanting to give success to their common cause. We would also represent that dissenters from the Church of England in this country have ever been desirous to conduct themselves as peaceable members of the civil government, for which reason they have hitherto submitted to several ecclesiastical burdens and restrictions that are inconsistent with equal liberty. But now when the many and grievous oppressions of our mother country have laid this continent under the necessity of casting off the yoke of tyranny and of forming independent governments upon equitable and liberal foundations, we flatter ourselves that we shall be free from all the encumbrances which a spirit of domination, prejudice, or bigotry has interwoven with most other political systems. This we are the more strongly encouraged to expect by the Declaration of Rights, so universally applauded for that dignity, firmness, and precision with which it delineates and asserts the privileges of society and the prerogatives of human nature, and which we embrace as the Magna Charta of our commonwealth that can never be violated without endangering the grand superstructure it was destined to sustain. Therefore, we rely upon this Declaration, as well as the justice of our honorable legislature, to secure us the free exercise of religion according to the dictates of our consciences; and we should fall short in our duty to ourselves, and the many and numerous congregations under our care, were we, upon this occasion, to neglect laying before you a state of the religious grievances under which we have hitherto labored that they no longer may be continued in our present form of government.

It is well known that in the frontier counties, which are justly supposed to contain a fifth part of the inhabitants of Virginia, the dissenters have borne the heavy burdens of purchasing glebes [parish land], building churches, and supporting the established clergy where there are very few Episcopalians either to assist in bearing the expense or to reap the advantage; and that throughout the other parts of the country, there are also many thousands of zealous friends and defenders of our state who, besides the invidious and disadvantageous restrictions to which they have been subjected, annually pay large taxes to support an establishment from which their consciences and principles oblige them to dissent—all which are confessedly so many violations of their natural rights, and, in their consequences, a restraint upon freedom of inquiry and private judgment.

In this enlightened age and in a land where all of every denomination are united in the most strenuous efforts to be free, we hope and expect that our representatives will cheerfully concur in removing every species of religious, as well as civil, bondage. Certain it is that every argument for civil liberty gains additional strength when applied to liberty in the concerns of religion; and there is no argument in favor of establishing the Christian religion but what may be pleaded, with equal propriety, for establishing the tenets of Mohammed by those who believe the Alcoran; or if this be not true, it is at least impossible for the magistrate to adjudge the right of preference among the various sects that profess the Christian faith, without erecting a chair of infallibility, which would lead us back to the Church of Rome.

We beg leave farther to represent that religious establishments are highly injurious to the temporal interests of any community. Without insisting upon the ambition and the arbitrary practices of those who are favored by government, or the intriguing, seditious spirit which is commonly excited by this as well as every other kind of oppression, such establishments greatly retard population, and consequently the progress of arts, sciences, and manufactories. Witness the rapid growth and improvements of the northern provinces compared with this. No one can deny that the more early settlement and the many superior advantages of our country would have invited multitudes of artificers, mechanics, and other useful members of society to fix their habitation among us, who have either remained in their place of nativity, or preferred worse civil governments and a more barren soil where they might enjoy the rights of conscience more fully than they had a prospect of doing it in this. From which we infer that Virginia might have now been the capital of America and a match for the British arms without depending on others for the necessaries of war, had it not been prevented by her religious establishment.

Neither can it be made to appear that the gospel needs any such civil aid. We rather conceive that when our blessed Savior declares His kingdom is not of this world, He renounces all dependence upon state power, and as His weapons are spiritual and were only designed to have influence on the judgment and heart of man, we are persuaded that if mankind were left in the quiet possession of their inalienable rights and privileges, Christianity, as in the days of the apostles, would continue to prevail and flourish in the greatest purity by its own native excellence and under the all-disposing providence of God.

We would humbly represent that the only proper

objects of civil government are the happiness and protection of men in the present state of existence; the security of the life, liberty, and property of the citizens; and to restrain the vicious and encourage the virtuous by wholesome laws; equally extending to every individual. But that the duty which we owe our Creator, and the manner of discharging it, can only be directed by reason and conviction, and is nowhere cognizable but at the tribunal of the universal Judge.

Therefore, we ask no ecclesiastical establishments for ourselves; neither can we approve of them when granted to others. This indeed would be giving exclusive or separate emoluments or privileges to one set (or sect) of men without any special public services to the common reproach and injury of every other denomination. And for the reasons recited, we are induced earnestly to entreat that all laws now in force in this Commonwealth which countenance religious domination may be speedily repealed, that all of every religious sect may be protected in the full exercise of their several modes of worship and exempted from all taxes for the support of any church whatsoever further than what may be agreeable to their own private choice or voluntary obligation. This being done, all partial and invidious distinctions will be abolished, to the great honor and interest of the State; and everyone be left to stand or fall according to merit, which can never be the case so long as any one denomination is established in preference to others.

That the great Sovereign of the universe may inspire you with unanimity, wisdom, and resolution, and bring you to a just determination on all the important concerns before you, is the fervent prayer of your memorialists.

Signed by order of the Presbytery.
John Todd, Moderator.
Caleb Wallace, P[resbytery] Clerk

∾ 6 ∾

Notes on the State of Virginia

Thomas Jefferson

Once the Revolution had commenced in earnest, Virginia became the principle American laboratory for the discussion of church-state relations. Lifting Virginia to preeminence in the church-state debate were the two men who, above all others, would give tongue to the American experiment (in the Declaration of Independence and Constitution). Of all the nation's founders, none were more fiercely committed to the achievement of unabridged religious liberty than Thomas Jefferson and James Madison, who sequentially would serve for sixteen years as president of the United States.

Jefferson considered the battle for religious freedom in Virginia "the severest contest in which I have ever been engaged." It began in 1776—when Jefferson returned to the Virginia House of Delegates from the Second Continental Congress in Philadelphia—and was not resolved until his "Statute for Establishing Religious Freedom" was enacted into law a decade later.

In 1779, at the age of thirty-six, Jefferson moved from the House of Delegates to the governor's office. His brief gubernatorial term was, to be charitable, undistinguished. In 1781, well before the Revolution had run its course, seeking a haven from the political fray, Jefferson retired to Monticello. There he composed his only book, *Notes on Virginia,* which includes the most complete statement of his opinions on religious freedom. Their publication—which would lead subsequent political opponents opportunistically to charge him with infidelity and even atheism—reconfirmed Jefferson's predisposition to keep religion a wholly private affair. "Religion is a subject on which I have ever been most scrupulously reserved," he wrote to Dr. Benjamin Rush of Philadelphia (an active Universalist layperson and cosigner of the Declaration of Independence). "I have considered it as a matter between every man and his Maker, in which no other, and far less the public, had a right to intermeddle."

On those rare occasions when Jefferson does entrust his inner thoughts on religion to a correspondent, he identifies himself most often as a Unitarian (though once, memorably, as "a sect unto myself").

Unitarians of the time routinely identified themselves as liberal or rational Christians; to what extent Jefferson considered himself to be a Christian is less clear. At most he was a nondoctrinal Christian, both nonsectarian and nonpracticing. His editing of the gospels (see my introduction to *The Jefferson Bible* [Beacon Press, 1989]) certainly suggests an irreverence to the letter of the scriptures, if not to their spirit. He believed in neither the Virgin Birth nor the Resurrection, excising both from his personal Bible. He also scorned the evangelists' "ignorance and chicanery" and considered St. Paul a theological charlatan. Yet, on more than one occasion, Jefferson expresses unbounded devotion to Jesus and his ethical teachings, which he held superior to those of all other ancient philosophers. He summed up his fidelity to Jesus in another letter to Dr. Benjamin Rush, who was among Jefferson's closest confidants on such matters: "I am a Christian in the only sense he wished any one to be; sincerely attached to his doctrines, in preference to all others; ascribing to himself every human excellence; and believing he never claimed any other."

One hundred and eighty years after his death, for all the attention that scholars have devoted to it, Jefferson's religious views remain as opaque as the man himself. His most telling definition of religion —"It is in our lives and not in our words that our religion must be read"—renders questions about what precisely he did believe, if not moot, less relevant than they might otherwise be. We can, however, identify one spiritual constant, running throughout Jefferson's entire adult life: his reverence for the principle of untrammeled religious liberty. Looking back on the birth of the nation and the principles upon which it was founded, Jefferson said to the University of Virginia Board of Visitors in 1819, "The constitutional freedom of religion [is] the most inalienable and sacred of all human rights." To speed its acceptance, Jefferson devotes his famous reflections on "Religion" in *Notes on Virginia,* which follow in their entirety.

❧ . . . . ❧

THE FIRST SETTLERS in this country [Virginia] were emigrants from England, of the English church, just at a point of time when it was flushed with complete victory over the religious of all other persuasions. Possessed, as they became, of the powers of making, administering, and executing the laws, they shewed equal intolerance in this country with their Presbyterian brethren, who had emigrated to the northern government. The poor Quakers were flying from persecution in England. They cast their eyes on these new countries as asylums of civil and religious freedom; but they found them free only for the reigning sect. Several acts of the Virginia assembly of 1659, 1662, and 1693, had made it penal in parents to refuse to have their children baptized; had prohibited the unlawful assembling of Quakers; had made it penal for any master of a vessel to bring a Quaker into the state; had ordered those already here, and such as should come thereafter, to be imprisoned till they should abjure the country; provided a milder punishment for their first and second return, but death for their third; had inhibited all persons from suffering their meetings in or near their houses, entertaining them individually, or disposing of books which supported their tenets. If no capital execution took place here, as did in New-England, it was not owing to the moderation of the church, or spirit of the legislature, as may be inferred from the law itself; but to historical circumstances which have not been handed down to us. The Anglicans retained full possession of the country about a century. Other opinions began then to creep in, and the great care of the government to support their own church, having begotten an equal degree of indolence in its clergy, two-thirds of the people had become dissenters at the commencement of the present revolution. The laws indeed were still oppressive on them, but the spirit of the one party had subsided into moderation, and of the other had risen to a degree of determination which commanded respect.

The present state of our laws on the subject of religion is this. The convention of May 1776, in their declaration of rights, declared it to be a truth, and a natural right, that the exercise of religion should be free; but when they proceeded to form on that declaration the ordinance of government, instead of taking up every principle declared in the bill of rights, and guarding it by legislative sanction, they passed over that which asserted our religious rights, leaving them as they found them. The same convention, however, when they met as a member of the general assembly in October 1776, repealed all *acts of parliament* which had rendered criminal the maintaining any opinions in matters of religion, the forbearing to repair to church, and the exercising any mode of worship; and suspended the laws giving salaries to the clergy, which suspension was made perpetual in October 1779. Statutory oppressions in religion being thus wiped away, we remain at present under those only imposed by the common law, or by our own acts of assembly. At the common law, *heresy* was a capital offence, punishable by burning. Its definition was left to the ecclesiastical judges, before whom the conviction was, till the statute c. 1 [1558] circumscribed it, by declaring, that nothing should be deemed heresy, but what had been so determined by authority of the canonical scriptures, or by one of the four first general councils, or by some other council having for the grounds of their declaration the express and plain words of the scriptures. Heresy, thus circumscribed, being an offence at the common law, our act of assembly of October 1777 (c. 17) gives cognizance of it to the general court, by declaring, that the jurisdiction of that court shall be general in all matters at the common law. The execution is by the writ *De haeretico comburendo* ["for the burning of a heretic"]. By our own act of assembly of 1705 (c. 30), if a person brought up in the Christian religion denies the being of a God, or the Trinity, or asserts there are more Gods than one, or denies the Christian religion to be true, or the scriptures to be of divine authority, he is punishable on the first offence by incapacity to hold any office or employment ecclesiastical, civil, or military; on the second by disability to sue, to take any gift or legacy, to be guardian, executor, or administrator, and by three years imprisonment, without bail. A father's right to the custody of his own children being founded in law on his right of guardianship, this being taken away, they may of course be severed from him, and put, by the authority of a court, into more orthodox hands. This is a summary view of that religious slavery, under which a people have been willing to remain, who have lavished their lives and fortunes for the establishment of their civil freedom.

The error seems not sufficiently eradicated, that the operations of the mind, as well as the acts of the body, are subject to the coercion of the laws. But our rulers can have authority over such natural rights only as we have submitted to them. The rights of conscience we never submitted, we could not submit. We are answerable for them to our God. The legitimate powers of government extend to such acts only as are injurious to others. But it does me no injury for my neighbour to say there are twenty gods, or no god. It neither picks my pocket nor breaks my leg. If it be said, his testimony in a court of justice cannot be relied on, reject it then, and be the stigma on him. Constraint may make him worse by making him a hypocrite, but it will never make him a truer man. It may fix him obstinately in his errors, but will not cure them. Reason and free enquiry are the only effectual agents against error. Give a loose to them, they will support the true religion, by bringing every false one to their tribunal, to the test of their investigation. They are the natural enemies of error, and of error only. Had not the Roman government permitted free enquiry, Christianity could never have been introduced. Had not free enquiry been indulged, at the era of the reformation, the corruptions of Christianity could not have been purged away. If it be restrained now, the present corruptions will be protected, and new ones encouraged. Was the government to prescribe to us our medicine and diet, our bodies would be in such keeping as our souls are now. Thus in France the emetic was once forbidden as a medicine, and the potatoe as an article of food. Government is just as infallible too when it fixes systems in physics. Galileo was sent to the inquisition for affirming that the earth was a sphere: the government had declared it to be as flat as a trencher, and Galileo was obliged to abjure his error. This error however at length prevailed, the earth became a globe, and Descartes declared it was whirled round its axis by a vortex. The government in which he lived was wise enough to see that this was no question of civil jurisdiction, or we should all have been involved by authority in vortices. In fact, the vortices have been exploded, and the Newtonian principle of gravitation is now more firmly established, on the basis of reason, than it would be were the government to step in, and to make it an article of necessary faith. Reason and experiment have been indulged, and error has fled before them. It is error alone which needs the support of government. Truth can stand by itself. Subject opinion to coercion: whom will you make your inquisitors? Fallible men; men governed by bad passions, by private as well as public reasons. And why subject it to coercion? To produce uniformity. But is uniformity of opinion desireable? No more than of face and stature. Introduce the bed of Procrustes then [that shrinks or stretches all to fit its length], and as there is danger that the large men may beat the small, make us all of a size, by lopping the former and stretching the latter. Difference of opinion is advantageous in religion. The several sects perform the office of a *Censor morum* ["control over public morals"] over each other. Is uniformity attainable? Millions of innocent men, women, and children, since the introduction of Christianity, have been burnt, tortured, fined, imprisoned; yet we have not advanced one inch towards uniformity. What has been the effect of coercion? To make one half the world fools, and the other half hypocrites. To support roguery and error all over the

earth. Let us reflect that it is inhabited by a thousand
millions of people. That these profess probably a
thousand different systems of religion. That ours is
but one of that thousand. That if there be but one
right, and ours that one, we should wish to see the
999 wandering sects gathered into the fold of truth.
But against such a majority we cannot effect this by
force. Reason and persuasion are the only practicable
instruments. To make way for these, free enquiry
must be indulged; and how can we wish others to indulge it while we refuse it ourselves. But every state,
says an inquisitor, has established some religion. No
two, say I, have established the same. Is this a proof
of the infallibility of establishments? Our sister states
of Pennsylvania and New York, however, have long
subsisted without any establishment at all. The experiment was new and doubtful when they made it.
It has answered beyond conception. They flourish in-
finitely. Religion is well supported; of various kinds,
indeed, but all good enough; all sufficient to preserve
peace and order: or if a sect arises, whose tenets would
subvert morals, good sense has fair play, and reasons
and laughs it out of doors, without suffering the state
to be troubled with it. They do not hang more male-
factors than we do. They are not more disturbed with
religious dissensions. On the contrary, their harmony
is unparalleled, and can be ascribed to nothing but
their unbounded tolerance, because there is no other
circumstance in which they differ from every nation
on earth. They have made the happy discovery, that

the way to silence religious disputes, is to take no notice of them. Let us too give this experiment fair play, and get rid, while we may, of those tyrannical laws. It is true, we are as yet secured against them by the spirit of the times. I doubt whether the people of this country would suffer an execution for heresy, or a three years imprisonment for not comprehending the mysteries of the Trinity. But is the spirit of the people an infallible, a permanent reliance? Is it government? Is this the kind of protection we receive in return for the rights we give up? Besides, the spirit of the times may alter, will alter. Our rulers will become corrupt, our people careless. A single zealot may commence persecutor, and better men be his victims. It can never be too often repeated, that the time for fixing every essential right on a legal basis is while our rulers are honest, and ourselves united. From the conclusion of this war we shall be going down hill. It will not then be necessary to resort every moment to the people for support. They will be forgotten, therefore, and their rights disregarded. They will forget themselves, but in the sole faculty of making money, and will never think of uniting to effect a due respect for their rights. The shackles, therefore, which shall not be knocked off at the conclusion of this war, will remain on us long, will be made heavier and heavier, till our rights shall revive or expire in a convulsion.

❧ 7 ❧

Memorial and Remonstrance Against Religious Assessments

James Madison

In 1776, when the Virginia House of Delegates postponed the thorny discussion of religious assessments to a later occasion, their resolution read, in part, as follows:

> [W]hereas great varieties of opinions have arisen touching the propriety of a general assessment or whether every religious society should be left to voluntary contributions . . . this difference of sentiments cannot now well be accommodated, so that it is thought most prudent to defer this matter to the discussion and final determination of a future assembly when the opinions of the country [Virginia] in general may be better known.

Whatever their views on the subject, no one at the time could have imagined that these matters would require a full decade to resolve.

By 1779, upon election as governor, Thomas Jefferson drafted and introduced essentially the same "Statute for Religious Freedom" that would finally pass in 1786. Before its final enactment, it languished for years in and out of committee, subject to endless nitpicking and wrangling. But if Jefferson's reforms were held in abeyance, so was the matter of assessments, with the temporary ban (first voted by the delegates in 1776) reissued yearly throughout the same period.

The legislation that finally broke the log-jam was not Jefferson's Statute, but Patrick Henry's call for a General Assessment, proposed upon his return to the House of Delegates (after succeeding Jefferson in the governor's office). In 1784, Henry's call for "A Bill Establishing a Provision for Teachers of the Christian Religion" galvanized the disparate elements in favor of reestablishing religion in Virginia. In league with such influential compatriots as future Supreme Court Chief Justice John Marshall and Revolutionary War hero Colonel Richard Henry "Lighthorse Harry" Lee, Patrick Henry's storied eloquence gave their common cause a stirring champion, even as his reputation as an advocate for religious liberty helped neutralize the arguments of anti-establishmentarians. Henry fashioned his bill in so inclusive a manner—

with state support promised to all Protestant factions— that even the Presbytery of Hanover issued
an initial letter of support. To accommodate the
Quakers and Mennonites (who had no ordained
ministers), the proposal included an alternate means
of support, underwriting the costs of worship rather
than the costs of clergy. Finally, to reassure his old allies in the battle for religious liberty, Henry explicitly
restated his full adherence to Article XVI in the Virginia Bill of Rights. In the late fall of 1784, with a 60
percent majority in favor, the House of Delegates ratified Henry's proposal in principle and sent it to a
drafting committee.

With Jefferson in Paris as American ambassador,
James Madison took charge swiftly, opportunistically
marshaling the opposition. Henry had argued that
his bill was necessary to support a renewal of morality and piety, both of which he felt had fallen into
decay. Among the bill's many advocates were promi-
nent Anglican clergymen, who—invoking for its
support "principles of public utility"—held that
Christianity presented the "best means of promoting
virtue, peace, and prosperity." Madison, a tactical as
well as analytical genius, turned these arguments in-
side out. He claimed that such a measure would instead undermine religion, even as it abridged liberty.
His strategy was to raise enough questions about the
moral merits of the case to table Henry's proposal,
giving him time to drum up popular opposition. This

strategy proved successful. The American church historian Edwin S. Gaustad notes, "The sweet reasonableness of Henry's proposal did not now, upon further reflection and with skillful Madisonian prodding, seem either so sweet or so reasonable after all."

Having raised sufficient concern to secure a one-year postponement, Madison made the most of his won time. First, he collaborated with his allies to move Patrick Henry back to the governor's office (which lessened Henry's influence over the legislature). Then, with the pressure off, popular mobilization against the measure could be—and was—generated across the state. To give but one example of the shifting climate of opinion, on further reflection the Hanover Presbytery reversed their earlier support and opposed the bill in 1785 as they had initially in 1776.

Not all advocates of religious liberty were convinced of the danger posed by state assessments, but Madison won many to his side nonetheless. George Washington (writing on October 3, 1785 to fellow Virginian George Mason) framed the debate as follows:

> Although no man's sentiments are more opposed to *any kind* of restraint upon religious principles than mine are, yet I must confess that I am not amongst the number of those who are so much alarmed at the thoughts of making people pay towards the support of that which they profess, if of the denomination of Christians; or

declare themselves Jews, Mahomitans or otherwise, and thereby obtain proper relief. As the matter now stands, I wish an assessment had never been agitated, and as it has gone so far, that the bill could die an easy death; because I think it will be productive of more quiet to the state, than by enacting it into a law, which, in my opinion, would be impolitic, admitting there is a decided majority for it, to the disquiet of a respectable minority. In the first case the matter will soon subside; in the latter, it will rankle and perhaps convulse.

Apart from the fascinating political intrigue that lies behind it, Madison's "Remonstrance" is an important document in its own right, one that has been cited in many court cases throughout the years. It was Jefferson not Madison who later employed the vivid metaphor of "a wall of separation between church and state." This "Remonstrance," however, together with Madison's insistence that Jefferson's Statute should guide the Constitution's framers on all matters referring to church-state separation, should leave no doubt regarding Madison's clear intentions with respect to the separation of church and state.

⌇ . . . . ⌇

WE THE SUBSCRIBERS, citizens of the said Commonwealth, having taken into serious consideration a bill printed by order of the last Session of General Assembly, entitled "A Bill Establishing a Provision for Teachers of the Christian Religion," and, conceiving that the same, if finally armed with the sanctions of a law, will be a dangerous abuse of power, are bound as faithful members of a free state to remonstrate against it, and to declare the reasons by which we are determined. We remonstrate against the said bill:

1. Because we hold it for a fundamental and undeniable truth, "that religion or the duty which we owe to our Creator and the manner of discharging it, can be directed only by reason and conviction, not by force or violence." The religion, then, of every man must be left to the conviction and conscience of every man; and it is the right of every man to exercise it as these may dictate. This right is in its nature an unalienable right. It is unalienable because the opinions of men, depending only on the evidence contemplated by their own minds, cannot follow the dictates of other men. It is unalienable, also, because what is here a right towards men is a duty toward the Creator. It is the duty of every man to render to the Creator such homage, and such only, as he believes to be acceptable to him. This duty is precedent both in order of time and degree of obligation to the claims of civil society. Before any man can be considered as a member of civil society, he must be considered as a subject of the Governor of the universe; and if a member of civil society who enters into any subordinate association must always do it with a reservation of his duty to the general authority, much more must every

man who becomes a member of any particular civil society do it with a saving of his allegiance to the universal sovereign. We maintain, therefore, that in matters of religion no man's right is abridged by the institution of civil society, and that religion is wholly exempt from its cognizance. True it is that no other rule exists by which any question which may divide a society can be ultimately determined than the will of the majority; but it is also true that the majority may trespass on the rights of the minority.

2. Because if religion be exempt from the authority of the society at large, still less can it be subject to that of the legislative body. The latter are but the creatures and vicegerents of the former. Their jurisdiction is both derivative and limited: it is limited with regard to the co-ordinate departments; more necessarily is it limited with regard to the constituents. The preservation of a free government requires not merely that the metes and bounds which separate each department of power may be invariably maintained, but more especially that neither of them be suffered to overleap the great barrier which defends the rights of the people. The rulers who are guilty of such an encroachment exceed the commission from which they derive their authority, and are tyrants. The people who submit to it are governed by laws made neither by themselves nor by an authority derived from them, and are slaves.

3. Because it is proper to take alarm at the first experiment on our liberties. We hold this prudent jealousy to be the first duty of citizens and one of the noblest characteristics of the late Revolution. The freemen of America did not wait till usurped power had strengthened itself by exercise and entangled the question in precedents. They saw all the consequences in the principle, and they avoided the consequences by denying the principle. We revere this lesson too much soon to forget it. Who does not see that the same authority which can establish Christianity, in exclusion of all other religions, may establish with the same ease any particular sect of Christians, in exclusion of all other sects? That the same authority which can force a citizen to contribute threepence only of his property for the support of any one establishment may force him to conform to any other establishment in all cases whatsoever?

4. Because the bill violates that equality which ought to be the basis of every law, and which is more indispensable, in proportion as the validity or expediency of any law is more liable to be impeached. "If all men are by nature equally free and independent," all men are to be considered as entering into society on equal conditions; as relinquishing no more, and therefore retaining no less, one than another, of their natural rights. Above all are they to be considered as retaining an "*equal* title to the free exercise of religion

according to the dictates of conscience." While we assert for ourselves a freedom to embrace, to profess, and to observe the religion which we believe to be of divine origin, we cannot deny an equal freedom to those whose minds have not yet yielded to the evidence which has convinced us. If this freedom be abused, it is an offense against God, not against man: To God, therefore, not to man must an account of it be rendered. As the bill violates equality by subjecting some to peculiar burdens, so it violates the same principle by granting to others peculiar exemptions. Are the Quakers and Mennonites the only sects who think a compulsive support of their religions unnecessary and unwarrantable? Can their piety alone be entrusted with the care of public worship? Ought their religions to be endowed above all others with extraordinary privileges by which proselytes may be enticed from all others? We think too favorably of the justice and good sense of these denominations to believe that they either covet preeminencies over their fellow citizens or that they will be seduced by them from the common opposition to the measure.

5. Because the bill implies either that the civil magistrate is a competent judge of religious truths, or that he may employ religion as an engine of civil policy. The first is an arrogant pretension falsified by the contradictory opinions of rulers in all ages and throughout the world; the second an unhallowed perversion of the means of salvation.

6. Because the establishment proposed by the bill is not requisite for the support of the Christian religion. To say that it is, is a contradiction to the Christian religion itself; for every page of it disavows a dependence on the powers of this world. It is a contradiction to fact, for it is known that this religion both existed and flourished not only without the support of human laws but in spite of every opposition from them; and not only during the period of miraculous aid but long after it had been left to its own evidence and the ordinary care of Providence. Nay, it is a contradiction in terms, for a religion not invented by human policy must have preexisted and been supported before it was established by human policy. It is, moreover, to weaken in those who profess this religion a pious confidence in its innate excellence and the patronage of its Author; and to foster in those who still reject it a suspicion that its friends are too conscious of its fallacies to trust it to its own merits.

7. Because experience witnesses that ecclesiastical establishments, instead of maintaining the purity and efficacy of religion, have had a contrary operation. During almost fifteen centuries has the legal establishment of Christianity been on trial. What have been its fruits? More or less in all places, pride and indolence in the clergy; ignorance and servility in the laity; in both, superstition, bigotry, and persecution. Inquire of the teachers of Christianity for the ages in

which it appeared in its greatest luster; those of every sect point to the ages prior to its incorporation with civil policy. Propose a restoration of this primitive state in which its teachers depended on the voluntary rewards of their flocks; many of them predict its downfall. On which side ought their testimony to have greatest weight, when for or when against their interest?

8. Because the establishment in question is not necessary for the support of civil government. If it be urged as necessary for the support of civil government only as it is a means of supporting religion, and it be not necessary for the latter purpose, it cannot be necessary for the former. If religion be not within the cognizance of civil government, how can its legal establishment be necessary to civil government? What influence in fact have ecclesiastical establishments had on civil society? In some instances they have been seen to erect a spiritual tyranny on the ruins of civil authority; in many instances they have been seen upholding the thrones of political tyranny; in no instance have they been seen the guardians of the liberties of the people. Rulers who wished to subvert the public liberty may have found an established clergy convenient auxiliaries. A just government, instituted to secure and perpetuate it, needs them not. Such a government will be best supported by protecting every citizen in the enjoyment of his religion with the same equal hand which protects his person and

his property; by neither invading the equal rights of any sect, nor suffering any sect to invade those of another.

9. Because the proposed establishment is a departure from that generous policy, which, offering an asylum to the persecuted and oppressed of every nation and religion, promised a luster to our country and an accession to the number of its citizens. What a melancholy mark is the bill of sudden degeneracy! Instead of holding forth an asylum to the persecuted, it is itself a signal of persecution. It degrades from the equal rank of citizens all those whose opinions in religion do not bend to those of the legislative authority. Distant as it may be, in its present form, from the Inquisition, it differs from it only in degree. The one is the first step, the other is the last in the career of intolerance. The magnanimous sufferer under this cruel scourge in foreign regions must view the bill as a beacon on our coast, warning him to seek some other haven, where liberty and philanthropy in their due extent may offer a more certain repose from his troubles.

10. Because it will have a like tendency to banish our citizens. The allurements presented by other situations are every day thinning their number. To superadd a fresh motive to emigration by revoking the liberty which they now enjoy would be the same species of folly which has dishonored and depopulated flourishing kingdoms.

11. Because it will destroy that moderation and harmony which the forbearance of our laws to intermeddle with religion has produced amongst its several sects. Torrents of blood have been spilled in the Old World [by] vain attempts of the secular arm to extinguish religious discord by proscribing all differences in religious opinion. Time has at length revealed the true remedy. Every relaxation of narrow and rigorous policy, wherever it has been tried, has been found to assuage the disease. The American theater has exhibited proofs that equal and complete liberty, if it does not wholly eradicate it, sufficiently destroys its malignant influence on the health and prosperity of the state. If, with the salutary effects of this system under our own eyes we begin to contract the bounds of religious freedom, we know no name that will too severely reproach our folly. At least let warning be taken at the first fruits of the threatened innovation. The very appearance of the bill has transformed "that Christian forbearance, love, and charity," which of late mutually prevailed, into animosities and jealousies, which may not soon be appeased. What mischiefs may not be dreaded should this enemy to the public quiet be armed with the force of a law?

12. Because the policy of the bill is adverse to the diffusion of the light of Christianity. The first wish of those who enjoy this precious gift ought to be that it may be imparted to the whole race of mankind. Compare the number of those who have as yet re-

ceived it with the number still remaining under the dominion of false religions; and how small is the former! Does the policy of the bill tend to lessen the disproportion? No, it at once discourages those who are strangers to the light of revelation from coming into the region of it; and countenances by example the nations who continue in darkness, in shutting out those who might convey it to them. Instead of leveling as far as possible, every obstacle to the victorious progress of truth, the bill, with an ignoble and unchristian timidity, would circumscribe it with a wall of defense against the encroachments of error.

13. Because attempts to enforce, by legal sanctions, acts obnoxious to so great a proportion of citizens tend to enervate the laws in general and to slacken the bands of society. If it be difficult to execute any law which is not generally deemed necessary or salutary, what must be the case where it is deemed invalid and dangerous? And what may be the effect of so striking an example of impotency in the government on its general authority?

14. Because a measure of such singular magnitude and delicacy ought not to be imposed without the clearest evidence that it is called for by a majority of citizens, and no satisfactory method is yet proposed by which the voice of the majority in this case may be determined or its influence secured. "The people of the respective counties are indeed requested to signify

their opinion respecting the adoption of the bill to the next session of Assembly." But the representation must be made equal, before the voice either of the representatives or of the counties will be that of the people. Our hope is that neither of the former will, after due consideration, espouse the dangerous principle of the bill. Should the event disappoint us, it will still leave us in full confidence that a fair appeal to the latter will reverse the sentence against our liberties.

15. Because, finally, "the equal right of every citizen to the free exercise of his religion according to the dictates of conscience" is held by the same tenure with all our other rights. If we recur to its origin, it is equally the gift of nature; if we weigh its importance, it cannot be less dear to us; if we consult the declaration of those rights which pertain to the good people of Virginia as the "basis and foundation of government," it is enumerated with equal solemnity, or rather, studied emphasis. Either then we must say that the will of the legislature is the only measure of their authority; and that in the plenitude of that authority; they may sweep away all our fundamental rights; or that they are bound to leave this particular right untouched and sacred. Either we must say that they may control the freedom of the press, may abolish the trial by jury, may swallow up the executive and judiciary powers of the state, nay, that they may despoil us of our very right of suffrage and erect themselves into an independent and hereditary assembly;

or we must say that they have no authority to enact into the law the bill under consideration. We, the subscribers, say that the General Assembly of this Commonwealth have no such authority. And...that no effort may be omitted on our part against so dangerous an usurpation, we oppose to it this remonstrance; earnestly praying, as we are in duty bound, that the Supreme Lawgiver of the universe, by illuminating those to whom it is addressed, may on the one hand turn their councils from every act which would affront His holy prerogative, or violate the trust committed to them; and on the other, guide them into every measure which may be worthy of His [blessing, may re]dound to their own praise, and establish more firmly the liberties, the prosperity, and the happiness of the Commonwealth.

❧ 8 ❧

Virginia Statute for
Religious Freedom

Thomas Jefferson

The broad public support that James Madison had generated with his "Remonstrance"—including petitions with thousands of signatures from all across Virginia—created a backlash of support for Thomas Jefferson's long-pending "Statute for Religious Freedom." Next to the Declaration of Independence, the Statute is Jefferson's most celebrated contribution to American statecraft. It also serves as the model for almost every subsequent state-sponsored confirmation of religious liberty, its eloquent phrases echoing in constitutions around the world.

Seizing upon the concern that arose in response to Patrick Henry's religious assessment bill, James Madison reintroduced Jefferson's "Statute" at the next full session of the House of Delegates. By a 67–20 vote, it won passage on January 16, 1786. Jefferson himself was out of the country at the time, serving the young nation as its ambassador to France. After receiving word of its passage and observing the public enthusiasm throughout Europe, Ambassador Jefferson proudly noted (in a letter posted from Paris on August 13, 1786, to John Wythe):

> Our act for freedom of religion is extremely applauded. The ambassadors and ministers of the several nations of Europe resident at this court have asked of me copies of it to send to their sovereigns, and it is inserted at full length in several books now in the press; among others, in the new Enclyclopedie. I think it will produce considerable good even in these countries, where ignorance, superstition, poverty, and oppression of body and mind in every form, are so firmly settled on the mass of the people....To know the worth of this, one must see the lack of it here.

Reflecting years later on the bill's passage, Jefferson's account of his long-awaited victory retains the tang of bitterness: "By unwearied exertions of Mr. Madison, in opposition to the endless quibbles, chicaneries, perversions, vexations, and delays of lawyers and demi-lawyers, [the bill] was passed by the legislature." His original text, drafted in 1779, did not survive unscathed by amendment. He lamented "some mutilations in the preamble," mostly small omissions that muted the expression of his personal philosophical convictions. One proposed amendment failed to pass, however. Where Jefferson's text reads, "the holy

73

author of our religion," some delegates thought it vital to qualify this by adding "Jesus Christ." As Jefferson recalls in his "Autobiography," "the insertion was rejected by a great majority, in proof that they meant to comprehend, within the mantle of its protection, the Jew and the Gentile, the Christian and Mahometan, the Hindoo, and Infidel of every denomination."

Jefferson considered his authorship of the "Statute for Establishing Religious Freedom in Virginia" one of three overridingly significant lifetime accomplishments. Together with his authorship of the Declaration of Independence and founding of the University of Virginia, he asked that it be carved on his gravestone (excluding, among many other notable acts of service, his two terms of service as president of the United States).

⇒ . . . . ⇐

I

WHEREAS ALMIGHTY GOD has created the mind free, that all attempts to influence it by temporal punishments or burdens, or by civil incapacitations, tend only to beget habits of hypocrisy and meanness, and are a departure from the plan of the Holy Author of our religion, who, being Lord both of body and mind, yet chose not to propagate it by coercions on either, as was in His almighty power to do; that the impious presumption of legislators and rulers, civil as well as ecclesiastical, who, being themselves but fallible and uninspired men, have assumed dominion over the faith of others, setting up their own opinions and modes of thinking as the only true and infallible, and as such endeavouring to impose them on others, has established and maintained false religions over the greatest part of the world, and through all time; that to compel a man to furnish contributions of money for the propagation of opinions which he disbelieves is sinful and tyrannical; that even forcing him to support this or that teacher of his own religious persuasion is depriving him of the comfortable liberty of giving his contributions to the particular pastor whose morals he would make his pattern and whose powers he feels most persuasive to righteousness, and is withdrawing from the ministry those temporary rewards which, proceeding from an approbation of their personal conduct, are an additional incitement to earnest and unremitting labors for the instruction of mankind; that our civil rights have no dependence on our religious opinions, any more than our opinions in physics or geometry; that, therefore, the proscribing of any citizen as unworthy of the public confidence by laying upon him an incapacity of being called to offices of trust and emolument unless he profess or renounce this or that religious opinion is depriving him injuriously of those privileges and advantages to which in common with his fellow citizens he has a natural right; that it tends only to corrupt the principles of that religion it is meant to encourage, by bribing with a monopoly of worldly honors and emoluments those who will externally profess and conform to it; that though indeed these are criminal who do not withstand such temptation, yet neither are those innocent who lay the bait in their way; that to suffer the civil magistrate to intrude his powers into the field of opinion, and to restrain the profession or propagation of principles on supposition of their ill tendency, is a dangerous fallacy which at once destroys all religious liberty, because he, being of course judge of that tendency, will make his opinions the rule of judgment, and approve or condemn the sentiments of others only as they shall square with or differ from his own; that it is time enough for the rightful purposes of civil government for its officers to interfere when principles break out into overt acts against peace and good order; and finally, that truth is great and will prevail if left to herself, that she is the proper and sufficient antagonist to error, and has nothing to fear from the conflict, unless by human interposition disarmed of her natural weapons, free argument and debate, errors ceasing to be dangerous when it is permitted freely to contradict them.

II

Be it therefore enacted by the General Assembly, That no man shall be compelled to frequent or support any religious worship, place, or ministry whatsoever, nor shall be enforced, restrained, molested, or burdened in his body or goods, nor shall otherwise suffer on account of his religious opinions or belief; but that all men shall be free to profess, and by argument to maintain, their opinion in matters of religion, and that the same shall in no wise diminish, enlarge, or affect their civil capacities.

III

And though we well know that this Assembly, elected by the people for the ordinary purposes of legislation only, have no power to restrain the acts of succeeding assemblies, constituted with powers equal to our own, and that therefore to declare this act to be irrevocable would be of no effect in law; yet as we are free to declare, and do declare, that the rights hereby asserted are of the natural rights of mankind, and that if any act shall hereafter be passed to repeal the present, or to narrow its operation, such act will be an infringement of natural right.

❧ 9 ❧

The Landholder, No. 7

Oliver Ellsworth

Until 1787, the church-state discussion had been waged primarily over religious liberty clauses in state constitutions and with respect to the assessment arrangements in states where religion was established (such as Massachusetts and Virginia). With the ratification of the U.S. Constitution, the debate went national, focusing on the constitutional proscription of religious tests for public office. At the time of the ratification debate, several colonies retained religious qualification for those seeking public office, requiring either that such candidates be Christian (Maryland and Massachusetts), Protestant (the Carolinas and New Jersey), or Trinitarian (Delaware).

The proposed Constitution—unlike the Declaration of Independence and almost all the state charters—made no mention of God whatsoever. This was not an oversight. Nor were mention of God and Christ deemed unnecessary, the Christian foundation for the new nation being so obvious. On the contrary, a spirited debate was waged over whether to bring God into the Constitution. Among several amendments proposed to rectify God's absence was one offered by a Connecticut delegate, who proposed that the preamble open as follows:

> We the people of the United States, in a firm belief of the being and perfections of the one living and true God, the creator and supreme Governor of the world, in his universal providence and the authority of his laws; that he will require of all moral agents an account of their conduct; that all rightful powers among men are ordained of, and mediately derived from God. . . .

When all was said and done, however, the Constitution contained only one reference to religion, providing, in Article VI, that "no religious test shall ever be required as a qualification to any office or public trust under the United States." In his *Commentaries on the Constitution of the United States,* Justice Joseph Story wrote, "This clause is not introduced merely for the purpose of satisfying the scruples of many respectable persons who feel an invincible repugnance to any religious test or affirmation. It had a higher object: to cut off forever every pretense of any alliance between church and state in the national Government." Isaac Backus celebrated the test clause in remarks before the Massachusetts Ratifying Convention. And, during the Virginia ratification debate, James Madison defended the exclusion of religious tests for office by reprising his now familiar argument in support of full religious liberty: "There is not a shadow of right in the general government to intermeddle with religion," he said. "Its least interference with it would be a most flagrant usurpation."

To ensure that the Constitution's meaning would be unmistakable, additions to the Constitution were proposed in New York, Pennsylvania, and Rhode Island (among other states) anticipating the language of the First Amendment ("Congress shall make no law respecting an establishment of religion, or prohibiting the free exercise thereof"). The prohibition of a religious test for office remained controversial, however. One North Carolina delegate considered it tantamount to "an invitation for Jews and pagans of every kind to come among us.... [T]hose gentlemen who formed this Constitution should not have given this invitation to Jews and heathens." In the New Hampshire Convention also, the want of a test clause led some to oppose ratification. In expressing his opposition, one delegate bemoaned that, due to the liberality of the Constitution's provisions, "a Turk, a Jew, a Roman Catholic, and what is worse than all, a Universalist, may be President of the United States." (His fears were soon realized, when Thomas Jefferson, at most a Unitarian, was elected president little more than a decade later.)

During the course of this debate, Connecticut signer of the Declaration of Independence Oliver Ellsworth published a stirring defense of the test clause (though he falls short of advancing complete religious freedom). Ellsworth was a member of the five man committee that drafted the Constitution at the Constitutional Convention in Philadelphia in 1787. Later a U.S. senator and third Chief Justice of the Supreme Court, Ellsworth gets credit for coining the term, "United States." He was also among the most vigorous and effective advocates for ratification, writing a series of public "Letters of a Landholder" to advance the cause. Ellsworth's argument in defense of the constitutional exclusion of religious tests for office appears in "Landholder No. 7" (published December 7, 1787). He speaks here not only as a lawyer, but also as a knowledgeable layman. He was active for decades in the First Congregational Church of Windsor, Connecticut; and, before turning to the study of law, Ellsworth's first degree from Princeton—shortly before John Witherspoon, Caleb Wallace, and James Madison's time there—was taken in theology.

SOME VERY WORTHY persons who have not had great advantages for information have objected against that clause in the Constitution which provides that no religious test shall ever be required as a qualification to any office or public trust under the United States. They have been afraid that this clause is unfavorable to religion. But, my countrymen, the sole purpose and effect of it is to exclude persecution and to secure to you the important right of religious liberty. We are almost the only people in the world who have a full enjoyment of this important right of human nature. In our country every man has a right to worship God in that way which is most agreeable to his conscience. If he be a good and peaceable person, he is liable to no penalties or incapacities on account of his religious sentiments; or, in other words, he is not subject to persecution.

But in other parts of the world it has been, and still is, far different. Systems of religious error have been adopted in times of ignorance. It has been the interest of tyrannical kings, popes, and prelates to maintain these errors. When the clouds of ignorance began to vanish and the people grew more enlightened, there was no other way to keep them in error but to prohibit their altering their religious opinions by severe persecuting laws. In this way persecution became general throughout Europe. It was the universal opinion that one religion must be established by law; and that all who differed in their religious opinions must suffer the vengeance of persecution. In pursuance of this opinion, when popery was abolished in England and the Church of England was established in its stead, severe penalties were inflicted upon all who dissented from the established church. In the time of the civil wars, in the reign of Charles I, the Presbyterians got the upper hand and inflicted legal penalties upon all who differed from them in their sentiments respecting religious doctrines and discipline. When Charles II was restored, the Church of England was likewise restored, and the Presbyterians and other dissenters were laid under legal penalties and incapacities.

It was in this reign that a religious test was established as a qualification for office; that is, a law was made requiring all officers, civil and military (among other things), to receive the sacrament of the Lord's Supper, according to the usage of the Church of England, [within] six months after their admission to office under the penalty of £500 and disability to hold the office. And by another statute of the same reign, no person was capable of being elected to any office relating to the government of any city or corporation unless, within a twelvemonth before, he had received the sacrament according to the rites of the Church of England. The pretence for making these severe laws, by which all but churchmen were made incapable of any office civil or military, was to exclude the Papists; but the real design was to exclude the Protestant dissenters. From this account of test laws, there arises an unfavorable presumption against them. But if we consider the nature of them and the effects which they are calculated to produce, we shall find that they are useless, tyrannical, and peculiarly unfit for the people of this country.

A religious test is an act to be done or profession to be made relating to religion (such as partaking of the sacrament according to certain rites and forms, or declaring one's belief of certain doctrines) for the purpose of determining whether his religious opinions are such that he is admissible to a public office. A test in favor of any one denomination of Christians would be to the last degree absurd in the United States. If it were in favor of either Congregationalists, Presbyterians, Episcopalians, Baptists, or Quakers, it would incapacitate more than three-fourths of the American citizens for any public office, and thus degrade them from the rank of freemen. There need be no argument to prove that the majority of our citizens would never submit to this indignity.

If any test act were to be made, perhaps the least exceptionable would be one requiring all persons appointed to office to declare, at the time of their admission, their belief in the being of a God, and in the divine authority of the Scriptures. In favor of such a test, it may be said that one who believes these great truths will not be so likely to violate his obligations to his country as one who disbelieves them; we may have greater confidence in his integrity. But I answer: His making a declaration of such a belief is no security at all. For suppose him to be an unprincipled man who believes neither the Word nor the being of God, and to be governed merely by selfish motives; how easy is it for him to dissemble! How easy is it for him to make a public declaration of his belief in the creed which the law prescribes and excuse himself by calling it a mere formality.

This is the case with the test laws and creeds in England. The most abandoned characters partake of the sacrament in order to qualify themselves for public employments. The clergy are obliged by law to administer the ordinance unto them, and thus prostitute the most sacred office of religion, for it is a civil right in the party to receive the sacrament. In that country, subscribing to the Thirty-Nine Articles is a test for administration into Holy Orders. And it is a fact that many of the clergy do this, when at the same time they totally disbelieve several of the doctrines contained in them. In short, test laws are utterly ineffectual; they are no security at all, because men of loose principles will, by an external compliance, evade them. If they exclude any persons, it will be honest men, men of principle who will rather suffer an injury than act contrary to the dictates of their consciences. If we mean to have those appointed to public offices who are sincere friends to religion, we, the people who appoint them, must take care to choose such characters, and not rely upon such cobweb barriers as test laws are.

But to come to the true principle by which this question ought to be determined: The business of a civil government is to protect the citizen in his rights, to defend the community from hostile powers, and to promote the general welfare. Civil government has no business to meddle with the private opinions of the people. If I demean myself as a good citizen, I am accountable not to man but to God for the religious opinions which I embrace and the manner in which I worship the Supreme Being. If such had been the universal sentiments of mankind and they had acted accordingly, persecution, the bane of truth and nurse of error, with her bloody axe and flaming brand, would never have turned so great a part of the world into a field of blood.

But while I assert the rights of religious liberty, I would not deny that the civil power has a right, in some cases, to interfere in matters of religion. It has a right to prohibit and punish gross immoralities and impieties; because the open practice of these is of evil example and detriment. For this reason, I heartily approve of our laws against drunkenness, profane swearing, blasphemy, and professed atheism. But in this state, we have never thought it expedient to adopt a test law; and yet I sincerely believe we have as great a proportion of religion and morality as they have in England, where every person who holds a public office must either be a saint by law or a hypocrite by practice. A test law is the parent of hypocrisy, and the offspring of error and the spirit of persecution. Legislatures have no right to set up an inquisition and examine into the private opinions of men. Test laws are useless and ineffectual, unjust and tyrannical; therefore the Convention have done wisely in excluding this engine of persecution, and providing that no religious test shall ever be required.

❧ 10 ❧

The Rights of Conscience

John Leland

A decade and a half before the American colonies declared their independence from Great Britain, 60 percent of the churches in the country were associated with Congregational and Anglican state establishments. Fifteen years after independence, that percentage had fallen by half, with as dominant a majority composed of dissenting communions. The spread of religious liberty, with an ever broader array of denominational choices available to church-shoppers, paralleled the achievement of political liberty in America.

As the new nation was defining itself during the debate over ratification, in his deservedly celebrated *Federalist No. 10,* James Madison presented the advantages of a free and competitive marketplace of ideas and interests in preventing any single faction or party to tyrannize over the entire body-politic. This principle obtains for religious diversity and competition as much as it does for any other kind. "In a free government, the security of civil rights must be the same as for religious rights," Madison writes. "It consists in the one case in the multiplicity of interests, and in the other, on the multiplicity of sects. The degree of security in both cases will depend on the number of interests and sects; and this may be presumed to depend on the extent of country and number of people comprehended under the same government."

Certainly the growing religious diversity in Virginia, with waves of New Light evangelists arriving throughout the 1760s and 1770s, speeded the establishment of religious freedom in that state. The Virginia struggle, in turn, helped frame the religious discussion during the debate over ratification in 1787. Among the dissenters who played a significant role in this discussion was John Leland, a twenty-three-year-old Baptist minister, who moved with his new wife from New England to Virginia in 1777. Apart from the gospel itself, Leland's primary passion was the cause of religious liberty. Looking back over nearly six decades of ministry, he summed up his life's work in these words: "Next to salvation of the soul, the civil and religious rights of men have summoned my attention, more than the acquisition of wealth or seats of honor."

One pivotal chapter of Leland's career took place during the debate over ratification of the Constitution. Initially, and strongly, he opposed ratification, because the Constitution lacked any explicit protection of religious liberty. If some Christians criticized the document for omitting all reference to God, Leland was sufficiently disappointed by the absence of a clear declaration of the rights of conscience initially to come out against ratification. His defection was no trivial matter. Leland's opposition and that of his fellow Baptists threatened to block the Constitution's passage in Virginia.

Leland lived in Orange county, where Madison (in absentia) was standing for delegate to the Virginia Ratifying Convention. Sensing trouble at home, Madison's father counseled his son to return from New York at once, lest his handiwork be undone by the very citizens who once had been his closest allies. "The Baptists are now generally opposed to it," he warned. Madison received the same message from his friend, James Gordon, Jr., who, together with Madison, made up the "pro" slate bidding to fill Orange County's two available seats at the Virginia convention. Writing on February 17, Gordon said:

> The sentiments of the people of Orange are much divided. The best men, in my judgement, are for the constitution, but several of those who have much weight with the people are opposed—Parson Bledsoe and Leeland, with Col. Z. Burnley. Upon the whole I think it is incumbent on you without delay to repair to this state,

as the loss of the constitution in this state may involve consequences the most alarming to every citizen in America.

Their mutual neighbor, Captain Joseph Spencer, fingered Leland as the principle antagonist. He sent Madison a list of Leland's objections—above all, the absence of a Bill of Rights to ensure complete religious liberty— and urged him to pay Elder Leland a visit as quickly as possible.

Shortly before the election, the two men met, with Leland sharing his concerns. Whatever transpired at that meeting, Leland ended up voting for ratification; Madison and Gordon won their seats handily; Virginia ratified the Constitution; and Madison went on to compose the Bill of Rights. Near his life's close, Leland recalled his historic meeting with the future president, noting, "When the Constitution first made its appearance in the autumn of 1787, I read it with close attention, and finally gave my vote for its adoption; and after the amendments took place, I esteemed it as good a skeleton as could well be formed."

Initially Madison had been opposed to any language in the Constitution guaranteeing religious liberty, on the assumption that these rights were covered implicitly and any amendment intended to make them explicit might be subject to compromise. "I am sure that the rights of conscience in particular, if submitted to public definition would be narrowed," Madison wrote. Thomas Jefferson disagreed. "I will tell you now what I don't like," he wrote to Madison from Paris. "First the omission of a bill of rights providing clearly and without the aid of sophisms for freedom of religion."

Soon, the combined concern of people like Jefferson (from the secular side) and Leland (from the religious) prevailed to change Madison's mind. On January 2, 1788, he wrote to another local Baptist minister (George Eve), "It is my sincere opinion that the Constitution ought to be revised, and that the first Congress meeting under it ought to prepare and recommend to the states for ratification, the most satisfactory provisions for all essential rights, particularly the rights of conscience in the fullest latitude."

In the first session of Congress, as promised, Madison helped draw up a Bill of Rights, submitting draft wording for what would become the First Amendment: "The civil rights of none shall be abridged on account of religious belief or worship, nor shall any national religion be established, nor shall the full and equal rights of conscience be in any manner, or on any pretext, infringed." These words were condensed to the now familiar formulation with which, in Article I, the Bill of Rights opens:

> Congress shall make no law respecting an establishment of religion, or prohibiting the free exercise thereof or abridging the freedom of speech, or of the press; or the right of the people peaceably to assemble, and to petition the Government for a redress of grievances.

With the First Amendment, James Madison's long struggle for freedom of conscience and church-state separation reached full fruition. To invoke the telling title of William Lee Miller's groundbreaking book on the subject, he enshrined religious freedom as *The First Liberty*.

In 1790, John Leland left Virginia for Connecticut, where he wrote two lengthy tracts: first, a chronicle of his time in Virginia; and, then, published the following year, "Rights of Conscience Inalienable, and Therefore, Religious Opinions Not Cognizable By The Law," a widely circulated broadside aimed at two of the final three standing state religious establishments (Connecticut and Massachusetts, the third being New Hampshire). In the former tract, he said:

> The notion of a Christian commonwealth should be exploded forever. . . . Government should protect every man in thinking and speaking freely, and see that one does not abuse another. The liberty I contend for is more than toleration. The very idea of toleration is despicable; it supposes that some have a pre-eminence above the rest to grant indulgence, whereas all should be equally free, Jews, Turks, Pagans and Christians.

The latter, an excerpt of which follows, is Leland's most sustained defense of religious liberty. In it, he draws directly from Jefferson's *Notes on Virginia*, echoing his arguments and sometimes even his language (for instance, Jefferson's claim that "It does me no injury for my neighbor to say there are twenty gods, or no god"). Leland returned to his home state in 1791, settling in Cheshire, Massachusetts where he served as pastor of the Second Baptist Church for the better part of fifty years until his death at eighty-seven in 1841.

⇒ . . . . ⇐

THE QUESTION IS, "Are the rights of conscience alienable, or inalienable?"

The word *conscience* signifies *common science*, a court of judicature which the Almighty has erected in every human breast: a *censor morum* over all his conduct. Conscience will ever judge right, when it is rightly informed, and speak the truth when it understands it. But to advert to the question, "Does a man upon entering into social compact surrender his conscience to that society to be controlled by the laws thereof, or can he in justice assist in making laws to bind his children's consciences before they are born?" I judge not, for the following reasons:

1. Every man must give an account of himself to God, and therefore every man ought to be at liberty to serve God in that way that he can best reconcile it to his conscience. If government can answer for individuals at the day of judgment, let men be controlled by it in religious matters; otherwise let men be free.

2. It would be sinful for a man to surrender that to man which is to be kept sacred for God. A man's mind

should be always open to conviction, and an honest man will receive that doctrine which appears the best demonstrated; and what is more common than for the best of men to change their minds? Such are the prejudices of the mind, and such the force of tradition, that a man who never alters his mind is either very weak or very stubborn. How painful then must it be to an honest heart to be bound to observe the principles of his former belief, after he is convinced of their imbecility; and this ever has been and ever will be the case while the rights of conscience are considered alienable.

3. But supposing it was right for a man to bind his own conscience, yet surely it is very iniquitous to bind the consciences of his children; to make fetters for them before they are born is very cruel. And yet such has been the conduct of men in almost all ages that their children have been bound to believe and worship as their fathers did, or suffer shame, loss, and sometimes life; and at best to be called dissenters, because they dissent from that which they never joined voluntarily. Such conduct in parents is worse than that of the father of Hannibal who imposed an oath upon his son while a child never to be at peace with the Romans.

4. Finally, religion is a matter between God and individuals, religious opinions of men not being the objects of civil government nor in any way under its control.

It has often been observed by the friends of religious establishment by human laws that no state can long continue without it; that religion will perish, and nothing but infidelity and atheism prevail.

Are these things facts? Did not the Christian religion prevail during the first three centuries in a more glorious manner than ever it has since, not only without the aid of law, but in opposition to all the laws of haughty monarchs? And did not religion receive a deadly wound by being fostered in the arms of civil power and regulated by law? These things are so.

From that day to this we have but a few instances of religious liberty to judge by; for in almost all states civil rulers (by the instigation of covetous priests) have undertaken to steady the ark of religion by human laws; but yet we have a few of them without leaving our own land.

The state of Rhode Island has stood above 160 years without any religious establishment. The state of New York never had any. New Jersey claims the same. Pennsylvania has also stood from its first settlement until now upon a liberal foundation; and if agriculture, the mechanical arts, and commerce have not flourished in these states equal to any of the states I judge wrong.

It may further be observed that all the states now in union, saving two or three in New England, have no legal force used about religion, in directing its course or supporting its preachers. And moreover the federal government is forbidden by the Constitution to make any laws establishing any kind of religion. If religion cannot stand, therefore, without the aid of law, it is likely to fall soon in our nation, except in Connecticut and Massachusetts.

To say that "religion cannot stand without a state establishment" is not only contrary to fact, but is a contradiction in phrase. Religion must have stood a time before any law could have been made about it; and if it did stand almost 300 years without law it can still stand without it.

The evils of such an establishment are many.

1. Uninspired fallible men make their own opinions tests of orthodoxy, and use their own systems, as Procrustes used his iron bedstead, to stretch and measure the consciences of all others by. Where no toleration is granted to non-conformists, either ignorance and superstition prevail or persecution rages; and if toleration is granted to restricted non-conformists, the minds of men are biased to embrace that religion which is favored and pampered by law (and thereby hypocrisy is nourished), while those who cannot stretch their consciences to believe anything and everything in the established creed are treated with contempt and opprobrious names; and by such means some are pampered to death by largesses and others confined from doing what good they otherwise could by penury. The first lie under a temptation to flatter the ruling party, to continue that form of government

which brings the sure bread of idleness; the last to despise that government and those rulers that oppress them. The first have their eyes shut to all further light that would alter the religious machine; the last are always seeking new light, and often fall into enthusiasm. Such are the natural evils of establishment in religion by human laws.

2. Such establishments not only wean and alienate the affections of one from another on account of the different usages they receive in their religious sentiments, but are also very impolitic, especially in new countries; for what encouragement can strangers have to migrate with their arts and wealth into a state, where they cannot enjoy their religious sentiments without exposing themselves to the law, when at the same time their religious opinions do not lead them to be mutinous? And further, how often have kingdoms and states been greatly weakened by religious tests! In the time of the persecution in France not less than 20,000 people fled for the enjoyment of religious liberty.

3. These establishments metamorphose the church into a creature, and religion into a principle of state, which has a natural tendency to make men conclude that *Bible religion* is nothing but a *trick of state*. Hence it is that the greatest part of the well-informed in literature are overrun with deism and infidelity; nor is

it likely that it will ever be any better while preaching is made a trade of emolument. And if there is no difference between *Bible religion* and *state religion*, I shall soon fall into infidelity.

4. There are no two kingdoms and states that establish the same creed or formularies of faith.... In one kingdom a man is condemned for not believing a doctrine that he would be condemned for believing in another kingdom. Both of these establishments cannot be right—but both of them can be, and surely are, wrong.

5. The nature of such establishments, further, is to keep from civil office the best of men. Good men cannot believe what they cannot believe; and they will not subscribe to what they disbelieve, and take an oath to maintain what they conclude is error: and as the best of men differ in judgment there may be some of them in any state: their talents and virtue entitle them to fill the most important posts, yet because they differ from the established creed of the state, they cannot—will not—fill those posts. Whereas villains make no scruple to take any oath.

If these and many more evils attend such establishments, what were and still are the causes that ever there should be a state establishment of religion? The causes are many—some of them follow.

1. The love of importance is a general evil. It is natural to men to dictate for others; they chose to command the bushel and use the whiprow, to have the halter around the necks of others to hang them at pleasure.

2. An over-fondess for a particular system or sect. This gave rise to the first human establishment of religion, by Constantine the Great. Being converted to the Christian system, he established it in the Roman Empire, compelled the pagans to submit, and banished the Christian heretics, built fine chapels at public expense, and forced large stipends for the preachers. All this was done out of love to the Christian religion: but his love operated inadvertently; for he did the Christian church more harm than all the persecuting emperors did. It is said that in his day a voice was heard from Heaven, saying, "Now is poison spewed into the churches." If this voice was not heard, it nevertheless was a truth; for from that day to this, the Christian religion has been made a stirrup to mount the steed of popularity, wealth, and ambition.

3. To produce uniformity in religion is another evil. Rulers often fear that if they leave every man to think, speak, and worship as he pleases, the whole cause will be wrecked in diversity; to prevent which they establish some standard of orthodoxy to effect uniformity. But is uniformity attainable? Millions of

JOHN LELAND

men, women, and children have been tortured to death to produce uniformity, and yet the world has not advanced one inch towards it. And as long as men live in different parts of the world, have different habits, education, and interests, they will be different in judgment, humanly speaking.

Is conformity of sentiments in matters of religion essential to the happiness of civil government? Not at all. Government has no more to do with the religious opinions of men than it has with the principles of the mathematics. Let every man speak freely without fear—maintain the principles that he believes—worship according to his own faith, either one God, three Gods, no God, or twenty Gods; and let government protect him in so doing (i.e, see that he meets with no personal abuse or loss of property for his religious opinions). Instead of discouraging him with proscriptions, fines, confiscation or death, let him be encouraged, as a free man, to bring forth his arguments and maintain his points with all boldness; then if his doctrine is false it will be confuted, and if it is true (though ever so novel) let others credit it. When every man has this liberty what can he wish for more? A liberal man asks for nothing more of government.

It is not supposable that any established creed contains the whole truth and nothing but the truth; but supposing it did, which established church has got it? All bigots contend for it—each society cries out,

"The temple of the Lord are we." Let one society be supposed to be in possession of the whole—let that society be established by law—the creed of faith that they adopt be so consecrated by government that the man that disbelieves it must die—let this creed finally prevail over the whole world. I ask what honor *truth* gets by all this? None at all. It is famed of a Prussian, called John the Cicero, that by one oration he reconciled two contending princes actually in war; but, says the historian, "it was his 6,000 horse of battle that had the most persuasive oratory." So when one creed or church prevails over another, being armed with (a coat of mail) law and sword, truth gets no honor by the victory. Whereas if all stand upon one footing, being equally protected by law as citizens (not as saints) and one prevails over another by cool investigation and fair argument, then truth gains honor, and men more firmly believe it than if it was made an essential article of salvation by law.

Truth disdains the aid of law for its defense—it will stand upon its own merits. The heathens worshipped a goddess called truth, stark naked; and all human decorations of truth serve only to destroy her virgin beauty. It is error, and error alone, that needs human support; and whenever men fly to the law or sword to protect their system of religion and force it upon others, it is evident that they have something in their system that will not bear the light and stand upon the basis of truth.

4. The common objection "that the ignorant part of the community are not capacitated to judge for themselves" supports the popish hierarchy, and all protestants as well as Turkish and pagan establishments, in idea.

But is this idea just? Has God chosen many of the wise and learned? Has He not hid the mystery of gospel truth from them and revealed it unto babes? Does the world by wisdom know God? Did many of the rulers believe in Christ when He was upon earth? Were not the learned clergy (the scribes) His most inveterate enemies? Do not great men differ as much as little men in judgment? Have not almost all lawless errors crept into the world through the means of wise men (so called)? Is not a simple man, who makes nature and reason his study, a competent judge of things? Is the Bible written (like Caligula's laws) so intricate and high that none but the letter-learned (according to common phrase) can read it? Is not the vision written so plain that he that runs may read it? Do not those who understand the original languages which the Bible was written in differ as much in judgment as others? Are the identical copies of Matthew, Mark, Luke, and John, together with the epistles, in every university and in the hands of every master of arts? If not, have not the learned to trust to a human transcription, as much as the unlearned have to a translation? If these questions and others of a like nature can be confuted, then I will confess that it is wisdom for a conclave of bishops or a convocation of clergy to frame a system out of the Bible and persuade the legislature to legalize it. No. It would be attended with so much expense, pride, domination, cruelty and bloodshed, that let me rather fall into infidelity; for no religion at all is better than that which is worse than none.

5. The groundwork of these establishments of religion is *clerical influence*. Rulers, being persuaded by the clergy that an establishment of religion by human laws would promote the knowledge of the gospel, quell religious disputes, prevent heresy, produce uniformity, and finally be advantageous to the state, establish such creeds as are framed by the clergy; and this they often do the more readily when they are flattered by the clergy that if they thus defend the truth they will become *nursing fathers* to the church and merit something considerable for themselves.

What stimulates the clergy to recommend this mode of reasoning is,

Ignorance—not being able to confute error by fair argument.

Indolence—not being willing to spend any time to confute the heretical.

But chiefly covetousness, to get money—for it may be observed that in all these establishments settled salaries for the clergy recoverable by law are sure to be interwoven; and was not this the case, I am well convinced that there would not be many if any religious establishments in the Christian world.

❧ 11 ❧

Letters on Religious Laws

George Washington

W hile the new nation's shape was being hammered out, George Washington largely stood
above the fray, a luxury he was permitted on account
of his iconic status as father of the nation. He took
particular care almost never to broach matters per-
taining to religion.

Washington's personal views on religion are ob-
scure. Though raised Anglican, he chose not to take
Communion (a rite reserved for church members or
"communicants"). When he attended church, he
was not particular about the house of worship—
attending Quaker, German Reformed, and Roman
Catholic services as well as those conducted by main-
line Protestants. He was just as inclusive in his

personal hiring, welcoming (in a letter to Tench Tighman, March 24, 1784) "Mohometans, Jews or Christians of any Sect, or they may be Atheists," so long as they "are good workmen." As commander-in-chief of the Revolutionary forces, Washington rejected a request by the other army chaplains to preclude John Murray, a Universalist minister, from serving in that capacity. Yet he encouraged his unit commanders to begin each day with a prayer. And, as president, he inaugurated the tradition—suspended by Jefferson, only to be reinstated by Madison—of issuing national prayers of thanksgiving.

Arguing from such evidence (buttressed by the fact that he knelt alongside his fellow delegates while an Episcopal priest recited the Thirty-fifth Psalm at the outset of the First Continental Congress), advocates for a Christian America place Washington at the head of their march. His general attitude toward religion does not support such a claim. At times, he even evinced a personal animus against organized religion. There are reports that after one preacher, with Washington captive in the pews, upbraided him for refusing communion—it being the duty of great men to set a good example—Washington never returned to church again.

On church-state separation, Washington is most forthcoming in a series of letters he wrote early in his presidency to religious leaders and congregations of various faiths. In them, he either pledges the government's absolute neutrality in matters of religion or defends that neutrality. In letters written in May 1789 (his first month in office), Washington reassured the United Baptist Church's General Committee that their rights were safe on his watch and issued a like promise to a conference of Methodist Bishops. That October, he made the same protections clear to the Quaker annual assembly for the Mid-Atlantic states, western Maryland, and Virginia. The following month, he gently, yet decisively, answered a complaint from the New Hampshire–Massachusetts Presbytery that no mention of either God or Christ had been included in the Constitution. Shortly thereafter, President Washington reached out to America's Roman Catholic and Jewish populations as well, in the latter instance assuring the warden of a Hebrew congregation in Newport, Rhode Island, that fines and imprisonment for breaking Christian sabbath statutes would now be a thing of the past.

Washington's commitment to church-state separation was unequivocal. For this reason, that religious animosities continued to prove divisive and sometimes seemed intractable frustrated him deeply. That frustration is evident in a letter he wrote to Sir Edward Newenham (Oct. 20, 1792):

> Of all the animosities which have existed among mankind, those which are caused by a difference of sentiments in religion appear to be the most inveterate and distressing, and ought most to be deprecated. I was in

hopes that the enlightened and liberal policy, which has marked the public age, would at least have reconciled Christians of every denomination ... that we should never again see their religious disputes carried to such a pitch as to endanger the peace of society.

❧ • ❧

I
To the Baptists
[May, 1789]

IF I COULD have entertained the slightest apprehension that the constitution framed in the convention, where I had the honor to preside, might possibly endanger the religious rights of any ecclesiastical society, certainly I would never have placed my signature to it; and, if I could now conceive that the general government might ever be so administered as to render the liberty of conscience insecure, I beg you will be persuaded, that no one would be more zealous than myself to establish effectual barriers against the horrors of spiritual tyranny, and every species of religious persecution—For you doubtless remember, that I have often expressed my sentiments, that every man, conducting himself as a good citizen, and being accountable to God alone for his religious opinions, ought to be protected in worshiping the Deity according to the dictates of his own conscience.

2
To the Methodists
[May 29, 1789]

IT SHALL STILL be my endeavor to manifest by overt acts, the purity of my inclinations for promoting the happiness of mankind, as well as the sincerity of my desires to contribute whatever may be in my power towards the preservation of the civil and religious liberties of the American People.

3
To the Quakers
[October, 1789]

GOVERNMENT BEING, among other purposes, instituted to protect the persons and consciences of men from oppression, it certainly is the duty of rulers, not only to abstain from it themselves, but, according to their stations, to prevent it in others. The liberty enjoyed by the people of these States, of worshipping Almighty God agreeably to their consciences, is not only among the choicest of their blessings, but also of their rights. While men perform their social duties faithfully, they do all that society or the state can with propriety demand or expect; and remain responsible only to their Maker for the religion, or modes of faith, which they may prefer or profess.

Your principles and conduct are well known to me;

and it is doing the people called Quakers no more than justice to say, that (except their declining to share with others the burthen of the common defence) there is no denomination among us, who are more exemplary and useful citizens.

I assure you very explicitly that, in my opinion the conscientious scruples of all men should be treated with great delicacy and tenderness; and it is my wish and desire, that the laws may always be as extensively accommodated to them, as a due regard to the protection and essential interests of the nation may justify and permit.

4
To the Presbyterians
[November 2, 1789]

THE TRIBUTE OF thanksgiving which you offer to "the gracious Father of lights" for his inspiration of our public-councils with wisdom and firmness to complete the national Constitution, is worthy of men, who, devoted to the pious purposes of religion, desire their accomplishment by such means as advance the temporal happiness of their fellow-men. And, here, I am persuaded, you will permit me to observe that the path of true piety is so plain as to require but little political direction. To this consideration we ought to ascribe the absence of any regulation, respecting religion, from the Magna Charta of our country.

To the guidance of the ministers of the gospel this important object is, perhaps, committed. It will be your care to instruct the ignorant, and to reclaim the devious; and, in the progress of morality and science, to which our government will give every furtherance, we may confidently expect the advancement of true religion, and the completion of our happiness.

5
To the Roman Catholics
[March, 1790]

AS MANKIND become more liberal, they will be more apt to allow, that all those who conduct themselves as worthy members of the community are equally entitled to the protections of civil government. I hope ever to see America among the foremost nations in examples of justice and liberality.

6
To the Jews
[August 18, 1790]

ALL POSSESS ALIKE liberty of conscience and immunities of citizenship. It is now no more that toleration is spoken of as if it was by the indulgence of one class of people, that another enjoyed the exercise of their inherent natural rights. For happily the government of the United States, which gives to bigotry no sanction, to persecution no assistance, requires only that they who live under its protection should demean themselves as good citizens, in giving it on all occasions their effectual support....

May the children of the Stock of Abraham, who dwell in this land, continue to merit and enjoy the good will of the other inhabitants, while every one shall sit in safety under his own vine and fig-tree, and there shall be none to make him afraid.

May the Father of all mercies scatter light and not darkness in our paths, and make us all in our several vocations useful here, and in his own due time and way everlastingly happy.

We have abundant reason to rejoice that in this Land the light of truth and reason has triumphed over the power of bigotry and supersti[ti]on, and that every person may here worship God according to the dictates of his own heart. In this enlightened age and in this Land of equal liberty it is our boast, that a man's religious tenets will not forfeit the protection of the Laws, nor deprive him of the right of attaining and holding the highest Offices that are known in the United States.

❧ 12 ❧

Farewell Address
(Selections)

George Washington

Among the most memorable of all presidential speeches, George Washington's "Farewell Address"—handed out to the Cabinet on September 14, 1796 near the close of his second term—is, in many ways, a political last will and testament. Initially drafted by James Madison in 1792 to commemorate Washington's proposed early retirement from the presidency, Washington gave the address a radical reworking four years later, when he did turn over his office. After sharing his new draft with Madison, he accepted Treasury Secretary Alexander Hamilton's offer to take the original and revised versions, together with some additional notes, and combine them into a single document. In consultation with John Jay (who collaborated with Hamilton and

Madison on the *Federalist Papers* and left the signature of his fine prose on many of the new nation's foundational documents), Hamilton cast the address in its present form, which Washington tightened up in a final edit.

Questions have been raised as to whether Washington's "Farewell" represents his own sense of priorities or those of Alexander Hamilton. Though Hamilton recast the address, giving it a more uplifting tone, the consensus is that Washington clearly is speaking here. Hamilton knew Washington's mind as well as anyone did. Furthermore, the president outlined his concerns for Hamilton, who omitted only the reference to education that Washington had been eager to include (and subsequently added, if in muted tones, to his own text). He also deleted several sentences that emphasized Hamilton's arch-Federalist views (for example, that the central government was in greater danger of becoming too weak than in being too strong). It is likely, however, that, without Hamilton's influence, Washington would not have included as many references to religion, if any at all. Whenever possible, he had avoided the subject. In his edit, Washington did temper Hamilton's religious certitude, reversing Hamilton's assertion that we ought not "to flatter ourselves that morality can be separated from religion," gently admitting instead that the opposite might possibly be true: "Let us with caution indulge the supposition that morality can be maintained without religion." On balance, however,

Washington's "Farewell Address" expresses his personal hopes and concerns upon leaving office.

Celebrating *E pluribus unum* ("out of many, one") as his principle theme, in each section of his "Farewell" Washington harmonizes Madison's vigilance on behalf of the rights of the many *(pluribus)* with Hamilton's equally eloquent advocacy of national unity *(unum)*. Though best remembered for its warnings against entangling alliances abroad and divisive factions at home, in this address Washington also commends religion and morality as aids to amity, the cultivation of which is key to the survival of national integrity. Whatever his personal beliefs may have been, Washington publicly fashioned himself "a faithful and impartial patron of genuine, vital religion." His impartiality is evident in the letters he wrote to various religious leaders; his faithfulness finds its most complete expression in the "Farewell Address."

Washington's aversion to faction extends to religious faction. In the letter (cited earlier) to Sir Edward Newenham, he wrote, "Religious controversies are always productive of more acrimony and irreconcilable hatreds than those which spring from any other cause." For this very reason, Washington remained steadfast in his fidelity to the separation of church and state. He did not, however, oppose an admixture of religion and politics. In the spirit of Unitarian John Adams's statement that "the happiness of a people and the good order and preservation of civil government essentially depend on piety, religion and morality," Washington believed that civil government must rest upon a strong moral and religious foundation, taking both words in an inclusive, non-sectarian sense. At its best, religion elevates the moral tone of the entire nation. Save when employed to divide one group of citizens from another, it could not but serve harmonic and uplifting ends—or so Washington believed.

Should modern day partisans be tempted to adduce his "Farewell Address" as implicitly sanctioning the idea of a Christian nation, they need look no further than Washington's collected writings to discover precisely the opposite to be true. With respect to his personal theology, at most Washington can be labeled a dispassionate Deist—positing his faith in God the "Grand Architect," Higher Cause," and "Supreme Dispenser of all Good." Throughout the entire twenty volumes of his papers and correspondence (both private and public), not once does he mention Jesus Christ.

As was true of his other immortal address ("The First Inaugural"), Washington did not deliver his "Farewell" in person, but it found wide distribution and met with great public acclaim (beginning with its publication in Philadelphia's *Daily American Advertiser* on September 19, 1796).

Friends and fellow-citizens:

In looking forward to the moment which is intended to terminate the career of my political life my feelings do not permit me to suspend the deep acknowledgment of that debt of gratitude which I owe to my beloved country for the many honors it has conferred upon me; still more for the steadfast confidence with which it has supported me, and for the opportunities I have thence enjoyed of manifesting my inviolable attachment by services faithful and persevering, though in usefulness unequal to my zeal. If benefits have resulted to our country from these services, let it always be remembered to your praise and as an instructive example in our annals that under circumstances in which the passions, agitated in every direction, were liable to mislead; amidst appearances sometimes dubious; vicissitudes of fortune often discouraging; in situations in which not unfrequently want of success has countenanced the spirit of criticism, the constancy of your support was the essential prop of the efforts and a guaranty of the plans by which they were effected.

Profoundly penetrated with this idea, I shall carry it with me to my grave as a strong incitement to unceasing vows that Heaven may continue to you the choicest tokens of its beneficence; that your union and brotherly affection may be perpetual; that the free Constitution which is the work of your hands may be sacredly maintained; that its administration in every department may be stamped with wisdom and virtue; that, in fine, the happiness of the people of these States, under the auspices of liberty, may be made complete by so careful a preservation and so prudent a use of this blessing as will acquire to them the glory of recommending it to the applause, the affection, and adoption of every nation which is yet a stranger to it.

Here, perhaps, I ought to stop. But a solicitude for your welfare which can not end but with my life, and the apprehension of danger natural to that solicitude, urge me on an occasion like the present to offer to your solemn contemplation and to recommend to your frequent review some sentiments which are the result of much reflection, of no inconsiderable observation, and which appear to me all important to the permanency of your felicity as a people. These will be offered to you with the more freedom as you can only see in them the disinterested warnings of a parting friend, who can possibly have no personal motive to bias his counsel. Nor can I forget as an encouragement to it your indulgent reception of my sentiments on a former and not dissimilar occasion.

Interwoven as is the love of liberty with every ligament of your hearts, no recommendation of mine is necessary to fortify or confirm the attachment.

The unity of government which constitutes you one people is also now dear to you. It is justly so, for it is a main pillar in the edifice of your real independence, the support of your tranquility at home, your peace abroad, of your safety, of your prosperity, of that very liberty which you so highly prize. But as it is easy to foresee that from different causes and from different quarters much pains will be taken, many artifices employed, to weaken in your minds the conviction of this truth, as this is the point in your political fortress against which the batteries of internal and external enemies will be most constantly and actively (though often covertly and insidiously) directed, it is of definite moment that you should properly estimate the immense value of your national union to your collective and individual happiness; that you should cherish a cordial, habitual, and immovable attachment to it; accustoming yourselves to think and speak of it as of the palladium of your political safety and prosperity; watching for its preservation with jealous anxiety; discountenancing whatever may suggest even a suspicion that it can in any event be abandoned, and indignantly frowning upon the first dawning of every attempt to alienate any portion of our country from the rest or to enfeeble the sacred ties which now link together the various parts....

Of all the dispositions and habits which lead to political prosperity, religion and morality are indispensable supports. In vain would that man claim the tribute of patriotism who should labor to subvert these great pillars of human happiness—these firmest props of the duties of men and citizens. The mere politician, equally with the pious man, ought to respect and to cherish them. A volume could not trace all their connections with private and public felicity.

Let it simply be asked, where is the security for property, for reputation, for life, if the sense of religious obligation *desert* the oaths which are the instruments of investigation in courts of justice? And let us with caution indulge the supposition that morality can be maintained without religion. Whatever may be conceded to the influence of refined education on minds of peculiar structure, reason and experience both forbid us to expect that national morality can prevail in exclusion of religious principle....

Observe good faith and justice towards all nations. Cultivate peace and harmony with all. Religion and morality enjoin this conduct. And can it be, that good policy does not equally enjoin it? It will be worthy of a free, enlightened, and at no distant period a great nation to give to mankind the magnanimous and too novel example of a people always guided by an exalted justice and benevolence. Who can doubt that in the course of time and things the fruits of such a plan would richly repay any temporary advantages which might be lost by a steady adherence to it? Can it be that Providence has not connected the permanent felicity of a nation with its virtue? The experiment, at least, is recommended by every sentiment which ennobles human nature. Alas! is it rendered impossible by its vices? ...

In offering to you, my countrymen, these counsels of an old and affectionate friend I dare not hope they will make the strong and lasting impression I could wish—that they will control the usual current of the passions or prevent our nation from running the course which has hitherto marked the destiny of nations. But if I may even flatter myself that they may be productive of some partial benefit, some occasional good—that they may now and then recur to moderate the fury of party spirit, to warn against the mischiefs of foreign intrigue, to guard against the impostures of pretended patriotism— this hope will be a full recompense for the solicitude for your welfare by which they have been dictated.

❧ 13 ❧

The Treaty of Tripoli,
Article 11

Although there is no mention of God or Christianity in the United States Constitution (the absence of which the New Hampshire–Massachusetts Presbytery lamented in their complaint to President Washington), the nominal or active Christian status of many founders has led subsequent generations of Christian advocates to claim that the United States was originally established as a "Christian nation." The most explicit evidence to the contrary is contained in the Barbary Treaties, signed in Tripoli on November 4, 1796 and ratified by the United States Senate on June 10, 1797.

Drawn up by American representatives to protect the country's merchant ships from Barbary pirates, the treaty was secured by payment of "forty thousand Spanish dollars, thirteen watches of gold, silver and pinsbach, five rings (three of diamonds, one of saphire, and one with a watch in it), one hundred and forty piques of cloth, and four caftans of brocade." In exchange for this ransom, the Kingdom of Tripoli promised to constrain the pirates under their jurisdiction from interfering with American shipping. "The Treaty of Peace and Friendship" was drafted in Arabic, signed by David Humphreys, the Commissioner Plenipotentiary of the United States of America (who was assigned to negotiate the treaties), and translated by his agent, Joel Barlow. The treaty went into effect immediately, certification pending "the final ratification of the president of the United States of America, by and with the advice and consent of the Senate of the United States."

Barlow's translation is far from a perfect copy of the Arabic original. Its most curious omission is the eleventh article itself, which does not appear in the Arabic at all. In its place is a letter from the Pasha that has little bearing on the treaty or its contents. But since Barlow's translation of the treaty is the document that President John Adams approved and the full Senate ratified, Article 11 (which follows, with its spelling uncorrected) stands as a clear expression of U.S. policy. Broadly distributed to papers across the land, it was published with the following preamble authorized by the chief executive:

Now be it known, That I John Adams, President of the United States of America, having seen and considered the said treaty do, by and with the advice and consent of the senate, accept, ratify, and confirm the same, and every clause and article thereof. And to the end that the said treaty may be observed and performed with good faith on the part of the United States, I have ordered it to be made public.

＊ . . . . ＊

Article II

AS THE GOVERNMENT of the United States of America is not in any sense founded on the Christian Religion,—as it has in itself no character of enmity against the laws, religion or tranquility of Musselmen,—and as the said States never have entered into any war or act of hostility against any Mehomitan nation, it is declared by the parties that no pretext arising from religious opinions shall ever produce an interruption of the harmony existing between the two countries.

∾ 14 ∾

A Wall of Separation

Thomas Jefferson

One wedge issue in the 1800 presidential election, which pitted John Adams against Thomas Jefferson, was Jefferson's personal faith (or lack thereof). Though both men were nominally Unitarian, Adams had always supported the church establishment in Massachusetts, whereas Jefferson led the fight for church-state separation in Virginia, making Adams far more congenial to those who believed that a "Christian nation" should have only Christian leaders. One pundit wrote, "my objection to [Jefferson's] being promoted to the Presidency is founded singly upon his disbelief of the Holy Scriptures; or, in other words, his rejection of the Christian Religion and open profession of Deism."

At first Jefferson's backers were defensive, citing allusions in his writings to a belief in God, but his argument in the *Notes on Virginia* that it makes no difference whether a person believes in no God or twenty gods undercut that appeal. It was when they reframed the argument, claiming that Adams's re-election could jeopardize the franchise of religious freedom in the country that the debate swung in Jefferson's favor. Not alone those who shared his Enlightenment views, but Baptists, Presbyterians, and other dissenters rallied to Jefferson's defense. Once again secular rationalists and evangelicals, the odd bedfellows who brought religious freedom to America in the first place, triumphed, this time at the polls.

In the fall of 1801, early in Jefferson's first term of office, the Baptist Association of Danbury, Connecticut wrote the president a letter expressing their concern that complete religious liberty was yet to be established in the constitutions of all the states, including their own. In his response (January 1, 1802), Jefferson cited the First Amendment, describing its provision that the government should "make no law respecting an establishment of religion, or prohibiting the free exercise thereof," as, in effect, "building a wall of separation between church and state."

Jefferson understood that states retained the right to fashion their own laws on such matters, the Constitution reserving to the states powers not delegated to the federal government. For this reason, in 1798, when serving as vice president, he lobbied the constitutional convention meeting in Kentucky to follow the national model in creating new statutes. "One of the amendments to the Constitution," Jefferson reminded them, "expressly declares that 'Congress shall make no law respecting an establishment of religion, or prohibiting the free exercise thereof, or abridging the freedom of speech, or of the press,' thereby guarding in the same sentence and under the same words, the freedom of religion, of speech, and of the press; insomuch that whatever violates either throws down the sanctuary which covers the others."

Throughout his years in office, Jefferson's personal religious views and steadfast opposition to church establishments fanned the ire of many in the New England clergy. Writing to his friend, Benjamin Rush, he memorably declared that the clergy "believe that any portion of power confided to me [as president] will be exerted in opposition to their schemes. And they believe rightly, for I have sworn upon the altar of God eternal hostility against every form of tyranny over the mind of man." Such a view was certainly congenial to most American Baptists, however—both the "eternal hostility" to church-state collusion, and the appropriateness of swearing this hostility "on the altar of God." Near the end of his second term as president, Jefferson confirmed his solidarity with another group of Baptists (from Baltimore, Maryland) with these words: "A recollection of our former vassalage in religion and civil government will unite the zeal of every heart, and the energy of every hand, to preserve that independence in both, which, under the favor of heaven, a disinterested devotion to the public cause first achieved, and a disinterested sacrifice of private interests will now maintain."

❧ . . . . ☙

*Letter from the Danbury Baptist
Association to President Jefferson*
October 7, 1801

SIR,

Among the many millions in America and Europe who rejoice in your election to office, we embrace the first opportunity which we have enjoyed in our collective capacity, since your inauguration, to express our great satisfaction in your appointment to the Chief Magistracy in the United States. And though the mode of expression may be less courtly and pompous than what many others clothe their addresses with, we beg you, sir, to believe that none is more sincere.

Our sentiments are uniformly on the side of religious liberty: that Religion is at all times and places a matter between God and individuals; that no man ought to suffer in name, person, or effects on account of his religious opinions, [and] that the legitimate power of civil government extends no further than to punish the man who works ill to his neighbor. But sir, our constitution of government is not specific. Our ancient charter, together with the laws made coincident therewith, were adapted as the basis of our government at the time of our revolution. And such has been our laws and usages, and such still are, so that Religion is considered as the first object of Legislation; and therefore what religious privileges we enjoy (as a minor part of the State) we enjoy as favors granted, and not as inalienable rights. And these favors we receive at the expense of such degrading acknowledgments, as are inconsistent with the rights of freemen. It is not to be wondered at therefore, if those who seek after power and gain, under the pretence of government and religion, should reproach their fellow men, [or] should reproach their Chief Magistrate, as an enemy of religion, law, and good order, because he will not, dares not, assume the prerogative of Jehovah and make laws to govern the Kingdom of Christ.

Sir, we are sensible that the President of the United States is not the National Legislator and also sensible that the national government cannot destroy the laws of each State, but our hopes are strong that the sentiment of our beloved President, which have had such genial effect already, like the radiant beams of the sun, will shine and prevail through all these States—and all the world—until hierarchy and tyranny be destroyed from the earth. Sir, when we reflect on your past services, and see a glow of philanthropy and goodwill shining forth in a course of more than thirty years, we have reason to believe that America's God has raised you up to fill the Chair of State out of that goodwill which he bears to the millions which you preside over. May God strengthen you for the arduous task which providence and the voice of the people have called you—to sustain and support you and your Administration against all the predetermined opposition of those who wish to rise to wealth and importance on the poverty and subjection of the people.

And may the Lord preserve you safe from every evil and bring you at last to his Heavenly Kingdom through Jesus Christ our Glorious Mediator.

> Signed in behalf of the Association.
> *Nehemiah Dodge*
> *Ephram Robbins*
> *Stephen S. Nelson*

President Jefferson's Reply

GENTLEMEN:

The affectionate sentiment of esteem and approbation which you are so good as to express towards me, on behalf of the Danbury Baptist Association, give me the highest satisfaction. My duties dictate a faithful and zealous pursuit of the interests of my constituents, and in proportion as they are persuaded of my fidelity to those duties, the discharge of them becomes more and more pleasing.

Believing with you that religion is a matter which lies solely between man and his God, that he owes account to none other for his faith or his worship, that the legislative powers of government reach actions only, and not opinions, I contemplate with sovereign reverence that act of the whole American people which declared that their legislature would "make no law respecting an establishment of religion, or prohibiting the free exercise thereof," thus building a wall of separation between church and state. Adhering to this expression of the supreme will of the nation in behalf of the rights of conscience, I shall see with sincere satisfaction the progress of those sentiments which tend to restore to man all his natural rights, convinced he has no natural right in opposition to his social duties.

I reciprocate your kind prayers for the protection and blessings of the common Father and Creator of man, and tender you for yourselves and your religious association, assurances of my high respect and esteem.

Thomas Jefferson

~~ Epilogue ~~

A Detached Memorandum

James Madison

S ometime after he stepped down from the presidency, James Madison penned a memorandum
pointing out inconsistencies between governmental
practice (especially with respect to the employment of
congressional and military chaplains) and the spirit
of First Amendment separation between church and
state. Written sometime after 1816, when he com-
pleted his second term as president, Madison's detached memorandum on ecclesiastical endowments
(included in a larger set of reflections on monopolies
and corporations) raises two questions, only one of
which he attempts to answer. First, why, if he was so
violently opposed to the practice (as being irreconcilable "with the pure principles of religious freedom")
did he not pursue his opposition to the congressional

and military chaplain programs during his years in office? Second, why did he succumb to public pressure and issue several national proclamations of prayer and thanksgiving as president, reversing Thomas Jefferson's principled precedent and reestablishing a practice that has otherwise continued throughout the nation's history.

As to the former question, it is hard to reconcile Madison's principled courage and perseverance during the long fight against assessments in 1779 and 1785 with his countenancing the government's use of tax dollars to employ clergymen during his administration. As to the latter, Madison carefully draws the same line that George Washington had drawn before him between invoking God in the most universal language possible and doing so in such a way that the president never becomes party to religious faction. To declare a day of fasting, prayer, or thanksgiving, was not to *demand* but only to *recommend* citizen participation. Even so, one is surprised to see Madison (whose views on both religion and church-state separation so closely follow those of his political mentor, Thomas Jefferson) risk the charge, however unfair, of mixing not only religion and politics, but also church and state. One presumes that his sensitivity to the national state of alarm occasioned by the outbreak of the War of 1812 prompted his receptivity to publish his first such prayer when the Congress—upon declaring war—requested that he do so.

Though neither question admits to a ready or

simple answer, Madison's undated memorandum nonetheless serves as a fitting summation of church-state questions during the years of our nation's founding. A vivid restatement of his unequivocal support for church-state separation, it came to light in the mid-1940s (when a group of Madison's detached memoranda were unearthed among his papers and published in the *William and Mary Quarterly*) and reprises remarkably well the story we have told here — not only its drama, but also its unfinished business.

⋙ • • • • • • • • • • • • • • • • • • • ⋘

THE DANGER OF SILENT accumulations & encroachments by Ecclesiastical Bodies have not sufficiently engaged attention in the U.S. They [the states] have the noble merit of first unshackling the conscience from persecuting laws, and of establishing among religious seas a legal equality. If some of the States have not embraced this just and this truly Xn [Christian] principle in its proper latitude, all of them present examples by which the most enlightened States of the old world may be instructed; and there is one State at least, Virginia, where religious liberty is placed on its true foundation and is defined in its full latitude. The general principle is contained in her declaration of rights, prefixed to her Constitution: but it is unfolded and defined, in its precise extent, in the act of the Legislature, usually named the Religious Bill, which passed into a law in the year 1786.

Here the separation between the authority of human laws, and the natural rights of Man excepted from the grant on which all political authority is founded, is traced as distinctly as words can admit, and the limits to this authority established with as much solemnity as the forms of legislation can express.

The law has the further advantage of having been the result of a formal appeal to the sense of the Community and a deliberate sanction of a vast majority, comprizing every sect of Christians in the State. This act is a true standard of Religious liberty: its principle the great barrier agst [against] usurpations on the rights of conscience. As long as it is respected & no longer, these will be safe. Every provision for them short of this principle will be found to leave crevices at least thro' [through] which bigotry may introduce persecution; a monster, that feeding & thriving on its own venom, gradually swells to a size and strength overwhelming all laws divine & human.

Ye States of America, which retain in your Constitutions or Codes, any aberration from the sacred principle of religious liberty, by giving to Caesar what belongs to God, or joining together what God has put asunder, hasten to revise & purify your systems, and make the example of your Country as pure & compleat, in what relates to the freedom of the mind and its allegiance to its maker, as in what belongs to the legitimate objects of political & civil institutions.

Strongly guarded as is the separation between Religion and Govt in the Constitution of the United

States, the danger of encroachment by Ecclesiastical Bodies may be illustrated by precedents already furnished in their short history.

The most notable attempt was that in Virga [Virginia] to establish a general assessment for the support of all Xn sects. This was proposed in the year [1784] by P.H. [Patrick Henry] and supported by all his eloquence, aided by the remaining prejudices of the Sect which before the Revolution had been established by law. The progress of the measure was arrested by urging that the respect due to the people required in so extraordinary a case an appeal to their deliberate will. The bill was accordingly printed & published with that view. At the instance of Col: George Nicholas, Col: George Mason & others, the memorial & remonstrance agst it was drawn up, [by Madison himself], and printed Copies of it circulated thro' the State, to be signed by the people at large. It met with the approbation of the Baptists, the Presbyterians, the Quakers, and the few Roman Catholics, universally; of the Methodists in part; and even of not a few of the Sect formerly established by law [Episcopalian]. When the Legislature assembled, the number of Copies & signatures prescribed displayed such an overwhelming opposition of the people, that the proposed plan of a genl assessmt was crushed under it: and advantage taken of the crisis to carry thro' the Legisl: the Bill above referred to, establishing religious liberty.

In the course of the opposition to the bill in the

House of Delegates, which was warm & strenuous from some of the minority, an experiment was made on the reverence entertained for the name & sanctity of the Saviour, by proposing to insert the words "Jesus Christ" after the words "our lord" in the preamble, the object of which would have been, to imply a restriction of the liberty defined in the Bill, to those professing his religion only. The amendment was discussed, and rejected [by votes of 66–38 and 56–35], the opponents of the amendment having turned the feeling as well as judgment of the House agst it, by successfully contending that the better proof of reverence for that holy name wd be not to profane it by making it a topic of legisl discussion, & particularly by making his religion the means of abridging the natural and equal rights of all men, in defiance of his own declaration that his Kingdom was not of this world. This view of the subject was much enforced by the circumstance that it was espoused by some members who were particularly distinguished by their reputed piety and Christian zeal.

But besides the danger of a direct mixture of Religion & civil Government, there is an evil which ought to be guarded agst in the indefinite accumulation of property from the capacity of holding it in perpetuity by ecclesiastical corporations. The power of all corporations, ought to be limited in this respect. The growing wealth acquired by them never fails to be a source of abuses. A warning on this subject is emphatically given in the example of the various Charitable establishments in G.B. [Great Britain], the management of which has been lately scrutinized. The excessive wealth of ecclesiastical Corporations and the misuse of it in many Countries of Europe has Long been a topic of complaint. In some of them, the Church has amassed half perhaps the property of the nation. When the reformation took place, an event promoted if not caused, by chat disordered state of things, how enormous were the treasures of religious societies, and how gross the corruptions engendered by them; so enormous & so gross as to produce in the Cabinets & Councils of the Protestant states a disregard, of all the pleas of the interested party drawn from the sanctions of the law, and the sacredness of property held in religious trust. The history of England during the period of the reformation offers a sufficient illustration for the present purpose.

Are the U.S. duly awake to the tendency of the precedents they are establishing, in the multiplied incorporations of Religious Congregations with the faculty of acquiring & holding property real as well as personal! Do not many of these acts give this faculty, without limit either as to time or as to amount! And must not bodies, perpetual in their existence, and which may be always gaining without ever losing, speedily gain more than is useful, and in time more than is safe! Are there not already examples in the U.S. of ecclesiastical wealth equally beyond its object and the foresight of those who laid the foundation of it! In the U.S. there is a double motive for fixing limits in this case, because wealth may increase not only from additional gifts, but from exorbitant advances in the value of the primitive one. In grants of vacant lands, and of lands in the vicinity of growing towns & cities the increase of value is often such as if foreseen, would essentially controul the liberality confirming them. The people of the U.S. owe their Independence & their liberty, to the wisdom of descrying in the minute tax of 3 pence on tea, the magnitude of the evil comprized in the precedent. Let them exert the same wisdom, in watching agst every evil lurking under plausible disguises, and growing up from small beginnings. *Obesta principiis* ["Resist the beginnings"].

Is the appointment of Chaplains to the two Houses of Congress consistent with the Constitution, and with the pure principle of religious freedom? In strictness the answer on both points must be in the negative. The Constitution of the U.S. forbids everything like an establishment of a national religion. The law appointing Chaplains establishes a religious worship for the national representatives, to be performed by Ministers of religion, elected by a majority of them; and these are to be paid out of the national taxes. Does not this involve the principle of a national establishment, applicable to a provision for a religious worship for the Constituent as well as of the representative Body, approved by the majority, and conducted by Ministers of religion paid by the entire nation?

The establishment of the chaplainship to Congs is

a palpable violation of equal rights, as well as of Constitutional principles: The tenets of the chaplains elected [by the majority shut the door of worship agst [against] the members whose creeds and consciences forbid a participation in that of the majority. To say nothing of other sects, this is the case with that of Roman Catholics & Quakers who have always had members in one or both of the Legislative branches. Could a Catholic clergyman ever hope to be appointed a Chaplain! To say that his religious principles are obnoxious or that his sect is small, is to lift the evil at once and exhibit in its naked deformity the doctrine that religious truth is to be tested by numbers or that the major sects have a tight to govern the minor.

If Religion consist in voluntary acts of individuals, singly, or voluntarily associated, and it be proper that public functionaries, as well as their constituents should discharge their religious duties, let them like their constituents, do so at their own expense. How small a contribution from each member of Cong would suffice for the purpose! How just wd it be in its principle! How noble in its exemplary sacrifice to the genius of the Constitution; and the divine right of conscience! Why should the expence of a religious worship be allowed for the Legislature, be paid by the public, more than that for the Ex. or Judiciary branch of the Gov?

Were the establishment to be tried by its fruits, are not the daily devotions conducted by these legal Ec-

clesiastics, already degenerating into a scanty attendance, and a tiresome formality!

Rather than let this step beyond the landmarks of
power have the effect of a legitimate precedent, it will
be better to apply to it the legal aphorism *de minimis
non curat lex* ["the law does not fret over tiny infrac-
tions"]; or to class it *cum "maculis quas aut incuria fudit,
aut humana parum cavit natura*k" [with "faults which
come from negligence, or which human nature lets
slip by"].

Better also to disarm in the same way the precedent of Chaplainships for the army and navy, than
erect them into a political authority in matters of
religion. The object of this establishment is seducing;
the motive to it is laudable. But is it not safer to adhere to a right principle, and trust to its consequences,
than confide in the reasoning however specious in
favor of a wrong one. Look thro' the armies & navies
of the world, and say whether in the appointment of
their ministers of religion, the spiritual interest of the
flocks or the temporal interest of the Shepherds, be
most in view: whether here, as elsewhere the political
care of religion is not a nominal more than a real aid.
If the spirit of armies be devout, the spirit out of the
armies will never be Less so; and a failure of religious
instruction & exhortation from a voluntary source
within or without, will rarely happen: if such be not
the spirit of armies, the official services of their
Teachers are not likely to produce it. It is more likely
to flow from the labours of a spontaneous zeal. The

armies of the Puritans had their appointed Chaplains; but without these there would have been no lack of public devotion in that devout age.

The case of navies with insulated crews may be less within the scope of these reflections. But it is not entirely so. The chance of a devout officer, might be of as much worth to religion, as the service of an ordinary chaplain (were it admitted that religion has a real interest in the latter). But we are always to keep in mind that it is safer to trust the consequences of a right principle, than reasonings in support of a bad one.

Religious proclamations by the Executive recommending thanksgivings & fasts are shoots from the same root with the legislative acts reviewed.

Altho' recommendations only, they imply a religious agency, making no part of the trust delegated to political rulers.

The objections to them are:

1. that Govts ought not to interpose in relation to those subject to their authority but in cases where they can do it with effect. An *advisory* Govt is a contradiction in terms.

2. the members of a Govt as such can in no sense be regarded as possessing an advisory trust from their Constituents in their religious capacities. They cannot form an ecclesiastical Assembly, Convocation, Council, or Synod, and as such issue decrees or injunctions addressed to the faith or the Consciences of

the people. In their individual capacities, as distinct from their official station, they might unite in recommendations of any sort whatever, in the same manner as any other individuals might do. But then their recommendations ought to express the true character from which they emanate.

3. They seem to imply and certainly nourish the errounious idea of a *national* religion. The idea just as it related to the Jewish nation under a theocracy, having been improperly adopted by so many nations which have embraced Xnity, is too apt to lurk in the bosoms even of Americans, who in general are aware of the distinction between religious & political societies. The idea also of a union of all to form one nation under one Govt in acts of devotion to the God of all is an imposing idea. But reason and the principles of the Xn religion require that all the individuals composing a nation even of the same precise creed & wished to unite in a universal act of religion at the same time, the union ought to be effected thro' the intervention of their religious not of their political representatives. In a nation composed of various sects, some alienated widely from others, and where no agreement could take place through the former, the interposition of the latter is doubly wrong.

4. The tendency of the practice, to narrow the recommendation to the standard of the predominant sect. The Ist proclamation of Genl Washington dated

Jany. 1. 1795 recommending a day of thanksgiving, embraced all who believed in "a supreme ruler of the Universe." That of Mr. Adams called for a Xn worship. Many private letters reproached the Proclamations issued by J. M. [Madison himself] for using general terms, used in that of Presit W—n [Washington]; and some of them for not inserting particulars according with the faith of certain Xn sects. The practice, if not strictly guarded naturally terminates in a conformity to the creed of the majority and a single sect, if amounting to a majority.

5. The last & not the least objection is the liability of the practice to a subserviency to political views; to the scandal of religion, as well as the increase of party animosities. Candid or incautious politicians will not always disown such views. In truth it is difficult to frame such a religious Proclamation generally suggested by a political State of things, without referring to them in terms having some bearing on party questions. The Proclamation of Pres. W. which was issued just after the suppression of the Insurrection in Penna and at a time when the public mind was divided on several topics, was so construed by many. Of this the Secretary of State himself, E. [Edmund] Randolph seems to have had an anticipation.

The original draught of that Instrument filed in the Dept. of State [is] in the hand writing of Mr Hamilton, the Secretary of the Treasury. It appears that several slight alterations only had been made at the suggestion of the Secretary of State; and in a marginal note in his hand, it is remarked that "In short this proclamation ought to savour as much as possible of religion, & not too much of having a political object." In a subjoined note in the hand of Mr. Hamilton, this remark is answered by the counter-remark that "A proclamation of a Government which is a national act, naturally embraces objects which are political" so naturally, is the idea of policy associated with religion, whatever be the mode or the occasion, when a function of the latter is assumed by those in power.

During the administration of Mr Jefferson no religious proclamation was issued. It being understood that his successor was disinclined to such interpositions of the Executive and by some supposed moreover that they might originate with more propriety with the Legislative Body, a resolution was passed requesting him to issue a proclamation.

It was thought not proper to refuse a compliance altogether; but a form & language were employed, which were meant to deaden as much as possible any claim of political right to enjoin religious observances by resting these expressly on the voluntary compliance of individuals, and even by limiting the recommendation to such as wished simultaneous as well as voluntary performance of a religious act on the occasion.

Of Liberty of Conscience and Civil Establishment of Religion

Richard Price

The English mathematician and Unitarian minister Richard Price wrote a retrospective on the American Revolution that contains a section on the advancements that were marked during its course with respect to the extension of liberty of conscience and mandates for church-state separation. Thomas Jefferson responded to its receipt by writing Price a warm letter of appreciation: "The copy of your observations on the American Revolution which you were so kind as to direct to me ... I have read ... with very great pleasure.... The happiness of governments like ours, wherein the people are truly the mainspring, is that they are never to be despaired of. When an evil becomes so glaring as to strike them generally, they arouse themselves, and it is redressed." Written in 1785, Price's observations show how early in our history others around the world were looking to the American experiment in religious freedom with vested interest and hope.

❦ . . . . ❦

IN LIBERTY OF CONSCIENCE I include much more than toleration. Jesus Christ has established a perfect equality among his followers. His command is, that they shall assume no jurisdiction over one another and acknowledge no master besides himself. It is, therefore, presumption in any of them to claim a right to any superiority or preeminence over their brethren. Such a claim is implied whenever any of them pretend to tolerate the rest. Not only all Christians but all men of all religions ought to be considered by a state as equally entitled to its protection as far as they demean themselves honestly and peacably. Toleration can take place only where there is a civil establishment of a particular mode of religion, that is, where a predominant sect enjoys exclusive advantages, and makes the encouragement of its own mode of faith and worship a part of the constitution of the state, but at the same time thinks fit to suffer the exercise of other modes of faith and worship. Thanks be to God, the new American States are at present strangers to such establishments. In this respect, as well as many others, they have shewn, in framing their constitutions a degree of wisdom and liberality which is above all praise.

Civil establishments of formularies of faith and worship are inconsistent with the rights of private judgment. They engender strife. They turn religion into a trade. They shoar up error. They produce hypocrisy and prevarication. They lay an undue byass on the human mind in its enquiries and obstruct the progress of truth. Genuine religion is a concern that lies entirely between God and our own souls. It is incapable of receiving any aid from human laws. It is contaminated as soon as worldly motives and sanctions mix their influence with it. Statesmen should countenance it only by exhibiting in their own example a conscientious regard to it in those forms which are most agreeable to their own judgments, and by encouraging their fellow-citizens in doing the same. They cannot as public men give it any other assistance. All besides that has been called a public leading in religion, has done it an essential injury, and produced some of the worst consequences.

The Church Establishment in England is one of the mildest and best sort. But even here what a snare has it been to integrity? And what a check to free enquiry? What dispositions favourable to despotism has it fostered? What a turn to pride and narrowness and domination has it given the clerical character? What struggles has it produced in its members to accommodate their opinions to the subscriptions and tests which it imposes? What a perversion of learning has it occasioned to defend obsolete creeds and absurdities? What a burden is it on the consciences of some of its best clergy who, in consequence of being bound down to a system they do not approve, and having no support except that which they derive from conforming to it, find themselves under the hard necessity of either prevaricating or starving? No one doubts but that the English clergy in general could with more truth declare that they do not, than that they do, given their unfeigned assent to all and everything contained in the Thirty-nine Articles and the Book of Common-Prayer; and yet, with a solemn declaration to this purpose, are they obliged to enter upon an office which above all offices requires those who exercise it to be examples of simplicity and sincerity. Who can help execrating the cause of such an evil?

But what I wish most to urge is the tendency of religious establishments to impede the improvement of the world. They are boundaries prescribed by human folly to human investigation, and inclosures which intercept the light and confine the exertions of reason. Let any one imagine to himself what effects similar establishments would have in philosophy, navigation, metaphysics, medicine or mathematics. Something like this took place in logick and philosophy while the *ipse dixit* [sayings] of Aristotle and the nonsense of the schools maintained an authority like that of the creeds of churchmen. And the effect was a longer continuance of the world in the ignorance and barbarity of the dark ages. But civil establishments of religion are more pernicious. So apt are mankind to

148

misrepresent the character of the Deity and connect his favour with particular modes of faith, that it must be expected that a religion so settled will be what it has hitherto been—a gloomy and cruel superstition bearing the name of religion.

It has been long a subject of dispute, which is worse in its effects on society, such a religion or speculative atheism? For my own part, I could almost give the preference to the latter. Atheism is so repugnant to every principle of common sense that it is not possible it should ever gain much ground or become very prevalent. On the contrary, there is a particular proneness in the human mind to superstition, and nothing is more likely to become prevalent. Atheism leaves us to the full influence of most of our natural feelings and social principles and these are so strong in their operation that in general they are a sufficient guard to the order of society. But superstition counteracts these principles by holding forth men to one another as objects of divine hatred, and by putting them on harassing, silencing, imprisoning and burning one another in order to do God service. Atheism is a sanctuary for vice by taking away the motives to virtue arising from the will of God and the fear of a future judgment. But superstition is more a sanctuary for vice by teaching men ways of pleasing God without moral virtue and by leading them even to compound for wickedness by ritual services, by bodily penances and mortifications, by adorning shrines, doing pilgrimages, saying many prayers, receiving absolution from the priest, exterminating heretics, etc. Atheism destroys the sacredness and obligation of an oath. But has there not been also a religion (so called) which has done this, by leading its professors to a persuasion that there exists a power on earth which can dispense with the obligation of oaths, that pious frauds are right and that faith is not to be kept with heretics?

It is indeed only a rational and liberal religion, a religion founded on just notions of the Deity as a being who regards equally every sincere worshipper, and by whom all are alike favoured as far as they act up to the light they enjoy, a religion which consists in the imitation of the moral perfections of an almighty but benevolent governor of nature, who directs for the best all events, in confidence in the care of his providence, in resignation to his will, and in the faithful discharge of every duty of piety and morality from a regard to his authority and the apprehension of a future righteous retribution. It is only this religion (the inspiring principle of every thing fair and worthy and joyful and which in truth is nothing but the love of God and man and virtue warming the heart and directing the conduct)—it is only this kind of religion that can bless the world or be an advantage to society. This is the religion that every enlightened friend to mankind will be zealous to promote. But it is a religion that the powers of the world know little of and which will always be best promoted by being left free and open.

I cannot help adding here that such in particular is

the Christian religion. Christianity teaches us that
there is none good but one, that is, God, that he wil-
leth all men to be saved, and will punish nothing but
wickedness, that he desires mercy and not sacrifice
(benevolence rather than rituals), that loving him
with all our hearts, and loving our neighbour as ourselves, is the whole of our duty, and that in every nation he that feareth him and worketh righteousness
is accepted of him. It rests its authority on the power
of God, not of man, refers itself entirely to the un-
derstandings of men, makes us the subjects of a kingdom that is not of this world, and requires us to
elevate our minds above temporal emoluments and to
look forwards to a state beyond the grave where a
government of perfect virtue will be erected under
that Messiah who has *tasted death for every man*. What
have the powers of the world to do with such a religion? It disclaims all connexion with them, it made
its way at first in opposition to them, and, as far as it
is now upheld by them, it is dishonoured and vilified.

The injury which civil establishments do to Christianity may be learnt from the following considerations.

First, the spirit of religious establishments is opposite to the spirit of Christianity. It is a spirit of pride
and tyranny in opposition to the Christian lowly
spirit, a contracted and selfish spirit, in opposition to
the Christian enlarged and benevolent spirit, the
spirit of the world in opposition to the Christian
heavenly spirit.

Secondly, religious establishments are founded on

a claim of authority in the Christian church which overthrows Christ's authority. He has in the Scriptures given his followers a code of laws to which he requires them to adhere as their only guide. But the language of the framers of church establishments is 'We have authority in controversies of faith and power to decree rites and ceremonies. We are the deputies of Christ upon earth who have been commissioned by him to interpret his laws, and to rule his church. You must therefore follow us. The Scriptures are insufficient. Our interpretations you must receive as Christ's laws, our creeds as his doctrine, our inventions as his institutions.'

It is evident that these claims turn Christ out of the government of his own kingdom and place usurpers on his throne. They are therefore derogatory to his honour and a submission to them is a breach of the allegiance due to him. They have been almost fatal to true Christianity and attempts to enforce them by civil penalties have watered the Christian world with the blood of saints and martyrs.

Thirdly, the difficulty of introducing alterations into church establishments after they have been once formed is another objection to them. Hence it happens that they remain always the same amidst all changes of public manners and opinions and that a kingdom even of Christians may go on for ages in idolatrous worship after a general conviction may have taken place that there is but one being who is the

proper object of religious adoration and that this one
being is that one only living and true God who sent
Christ into the world and who is his, no less than he
is our God and father. What a sad scene of religious
hypocrisy must such a discordance between public
conviction and the public forms produce?

At this day in some European countries the absurdity and slavish-ness of their hierarchies are seen and
acknowledged but, being incorporated with the state,
it is scarcely possible to get rid of them.

What can be more striking than the state of England in this respect? The system of faith and worship
established in it was formed above two hundred years
ago, when Europe was just emerging from darkness
and barbarity. The times have ever since been growing more enlightened, but without any effect on the
establishment. Not a ray of the increasing light has
penetrated it. Not one imperfection, however gross,
has been removed.

The same articles of faith are subscribed. The same
ritual of devotion is practised. There is reason to fear
that the absolution of the sick, which forms a part of
this ritual, is often resorted to as a passport to heaven
after a wicked life and yet it is continued. Perhaps
nothing more shocking to reason and humanity ever
made a part of a religious system than the damning
clauses in the Athanasian creed and yet the obligation
of the clergy to declare assent to this creed, and to
read it as a part of the public devotion, remains.

RICHARD PRICE

The necessary consequence of such a state of
things, is, that, fourthly, Christianity itself is dis-
graced and that all religion comes to be considered as
a state trick and a barbarous mummery. It is well
known that in some Popish countries there are few
Christians among the higher ranks of men, the religion of the state being in those countries mistaken for
the religion of the Gospel. This indeed shows a criminal inattention in those who fall into such a mistake,
for they ought to consider that Christianity has been
grievously corrupted and that their ideas of it should
be taken from the New Testament only. It is, however, so natural to reckon Christianity to be that
which it is held out to be in all establishments of it,
that it cannot but happen that such an error will take
place and produce some of the worst consequences.
There is probably a greater number of rational Christians (that is, of Christians upon enquiry) in England, than in all Popish countries. The reason is that
the religious establishment here is Popery reformed,
and that a considerable body dissent from it and are
often inculcating the necessity of distinguishing between the Christianity established by law and that
which is taught in the Bible. Certain it is that, till this
distinction is made, Christianity can never recover its
just credit and usefulness.

Such then are the effects of civil establishments of
religion. May heaven soon put an end to them. The
world will never be generally wise or virtuous or

154

happy till these enemies to its peace and improvement are demolished. Thanks be to God they are giving way before increasing light. Let them never shew themselves in America. Let no such monster be known there as human authority in matters of religion. Let every honest and peaceable man, whatever is his faith, be protected there and find an effectual defence against the attacks of bigotry and intolerance. In the United States may religion flourish. They cannot be very great and happy if it does not. But let it be a better religion than most of those which have been hitherto professed in the world. Let it be a religion which enforces moral obligations, not a religion which relaxes and evades them. A tolerant and catholic religion, not a rage for proselitism. A religion of peace and charity, not a religion that persecutes, curses and damns. In a word, let it be the genuine gospel of peace, lifting above the world, wanning the heart with the love of God and his creatures, and sustaining the fortitude of good men by the assured hope of a future deliverance from death, and an infinite reward in the everlasting kingdom of our Lord and Saviour.

From the preceding observations it may be concluded that it is impossible I should not admire the following article in the declaration of rights which forms the foundation of the Massachusett's constitution: 'In this state every denomination of Christians demeaning themselves peaceably and as good subjects of the commonwealth shall be equally under the protection of the law, and no subordination of any one sect or denomination to another shall ever be established by law.'

This is liberal beyond all example. I should, however, have admired it more had it been more liberal, and the words, *all men of all religions* been substituted for the words, *every denomination of Christians*.

It appears farther from the preceding observations that I cannot but dislike the religious tests which make a part of several of the American constitutions. In the Massachusett's constitution it is ordered that all who take seats in the House of Representatives or Senate shall declare 'their firm persuasion of the truth of the Christian religion'. The same is required by the Maryland constitution, as a condition of being admitted into *any* places of profit or trust. In Pennsylvania every member of the House of Representatives is required to declare that he 'acknowledges the Scriptures of the Old and New Testament to be given by divine inspiration'. In the state of Delaware, that 'he believes in God the Father, and in Jesus Christ his only Son, and in the Holy Ghost, one God blessed for evermore'. All this is more than is required even in England where, though every person however debauched or atheistical is required to receive the sacrament as a qualification for inferior places, no other religious test is imposed on members of parliament than a declaration against Popery. It is an observation no less just than common that such tests exclude only honest men. The dishonest never scruple them.

Montesquieu probably was not a Christian. Newton and Locke were not Trinitarians and therefore not Christians according to the commonly received ideas of Christianity. Would the United States, for this reason, deny such men, were they living, all places of trust and power among them?

Sources

1. Patrick Henry. *American State Papers and Related Documents on Freedom in Religion*, William Addison Blakely, ed. (Washington, D.C.: Review and Herald, 1949), 178–81.
2. Samuel Adams. *The Annals of America*, vol. 2 (Chicago: Encyclopaedia Britannica, 1776), 217–20.
3. a) Isaac Backus. "An Appeal to the Public," from *Isaac Backus on Church, State, and Calvinism* (Cambridge, MA: Harvard University Press, 1968), 340–43.
    b) Massachusetts Provincial Congress. Cf. Thomas Armitage, *A History of the Baptists* (New York: Brian Taylor, 1887), 786.
    c) Isaac Backus. To the Massachusetts Assembly, from *Annals of America* 2, 366.
4. a) Virginia Declaration of Rights. *Annals of America* 2, 432–33.
    b) Massachusetts Bill of Rights. *Annals of America* 2, 533.
5. Hanover Memorial. *American State Papers*, 103–5.
6. Thomas Jefferson. *Notes on the State of Virginia* (New York: Penguin, 1999), 163–67.
7. James Madison. *James Madison: Writings*, Jack N. Rakove, ed. (New York: Library of America, 1999), 29–36.
8. Thomas Jefferson. *Annals of America* 3, 53–54.
9. Oliver Ellsworth. *Annals of America* 3, 170–72.
10. John Leland. *Annals of America* 3, 445–49.

Sources

11. George Washington. *The Papers of George Washington: Presidential Series*, W. W. Abbot, ed. (Charlottesville: University Press of Virginia, 1976–79).

    a) "To the United Baptist Churches of Virginia," vol. 2, 423–25.

    b) "To the Bishops of the Methodist Episcopal Church," 2, 411–12.

    c) "To the Society of Quakers," 4, 265–69.

    d) "To the Presbyterian Ministers of Massachusetts and New Hampshire," 4, 274–77.

    e) "To Roman Catholics in America," 5, 299–300.

    f) "To the Hebrew Congregation in Newport, Rhode Island," 6, 284–86.

12. George Washington. *Annals of America* 3, 606–15.

13. Treaty of Tripoli. *Treaties and Other International Acts of the United States of America*, vol. 2, Hunter Miller, ed. (Washington, D.C.: Government Printing Office, 1931), 349–85.

14. Thomas Jefferson. *Thomas Jefferson: Writings*, Merrill Peterson, ed. (New York: Library of America, 1997), 509–10.

Epilogue: James Madison. *James Madison: Writings*, 759–66.

Appendix: Richard Price. *Richard Price and the Ethical Foundations of the American Revolution*, Bernard Peach, ed. (Raleigh Durham, N.C.: Duke Univ. Press, 1979), 194–200.

Acknowledgments

My gratitude goes out to Helene Atwan, publisher of Beacon Press, and Tom Hallock, associate publisher, for inspiring this collection; and to my editor, Joanne Wyckoff, who shepherded it so deftly and quickly to press. I am grateful to have been given the opportunity to expand here on two earlier books, Beacon's edition of *The Jefferson Bible*, to which I offer the introduction, and *The American Creed*, my recent "biography" of the Declaration of Independence. As I noted at the outset of the latter, if we forget our history, not only are we doomed to repeat it, but, just as perilously, we also are doomed to fail to live up to it.